Competences for School Managers

Derek Esp

KOGAN
PAGE

London • Philadelphia

The Management and Leadership in Education Series
Series Editor: Howard Green

Competences for School Managers Derek Esp
Educational Values for School Leadership Sylvia West

First published in 1993

Kogan Page Limited
120 Pentonville Road
London N1 9JN

British Library Cataloguing in Publication Data

A CIP record for this book is available from the British Library.

ISBN 0 7494 0817 0

Typeset by Saxon Graphics, Derby
Printed and bound in Great Britain by
Clays Ltd, St Ives plc

Contents

Series Editor's Foreword

The government's educational reforms have created an unprece-
dented rate of change in schools. They have also raised many
fundamental questions about the purpose of education and the nature
of school management and leadership. Similar changes are occurring
in many other educational systems throughout the world. There is an
urgent need for all of us with an interest in education to step back and
reflect on recent educational reforms, to reaffirm old truths and
successful practice where necessary, to sift out the best of the changes,
modifying or abandoning those which are a distraction from the central
purpose of schools: to ensure that an education of high quality is a
guaranteed opportunity for *all* our children and young people.

This series has been carefully conceived to satisfy the growing need
for short, readable books designed for busy people and with a focus on
issues at the cutting edge of school management and leadership.

They are written by reflective practitioners rather than theorists.
The authors include heads, advisers, inspectors, education officers,
trainers and governors who are working at the sharp end, trying to
make sense of the welter of change and with a common desire to
contribute to a strong and continually improving system of education
in the UK. The series celebrates the ideals, skills and expertise of
professionals in education who want to work in partnership with all the
other stakeholders in our schools.

In this book, Derek Esp provides an informative and practical
analysis of the use of management competences in education.
Competences have become firmly established as a framework for staff
development and selection in a wide range of organizations and
occupations, particularly through the work of the Management

Charter Initiative on management standards. In education, competences are now being used at several stages of the teaching profession from initial training to the preparation for headship. This reflects the fact that 'management' is a process as relevant to the teacher planning a series of lessons with a class as to the head preparing the school budget.

The book contains several case studies of the application of management competences, reviews the relevance of these models to the demands of self-managing schools and provides practical guidance about how competences may be applied in a variety of educational contexts. Derek Esp has written a most valuable introduction to this important topic which will be of interest to all those wishing to develop the link between competent staff and successful schools in a more systematic and rigorous manner.

Howard Green
Eggbuckland
October 1992

Preface

Many teachers consider 'management' to be a highly suspect word. They associate it with undue interference by bureaucrats at national, local authority and school level. The word 'competence' also summons up visions of faceless administrators grinding everything to grey powder.

I wrote this book in the belief that effective management is vital for effective pupil learning and imaginative teaching. The competent manager provides a positive, supportive environment for pupils and teachers alike. Competent managers are in the business of ensuring that teachers and pupils have the materials and equipment they require; that people are encouraged to give of their best; that personal and professional development is a natural part of the school 'climate' and that the work of every individual is valued and nurtured.

There is some resistance to the idea that competences can be identified and developed. This is not surprising. Much of what managers do is difficult to define and stems from their flair, initiative and creativity. Nevertheless managerial competences can be developed to the benefit of the individual and the school. The case studies in this book demonstrate the ways in which teachers are developing competences and improving their job satisfaction. They illustrate various approaches to the development of competences in the workplace.

I have been directly involved with two of the schemes described. I helped to establish the College of Preceptors ACP (Management) pilot scheme. I also evaluated, with Malcolm Young, the first phase of the National Educational Assessment Centre project. This has given me direct experience of hearing about the benefits of competence-based professional development from experienced teachers, their tutors and mentors. These are not starry-eyed idealists. They have applied competences critically and analytically and have found them to be of practical benefit in their day-to-day work.

As with any other new development, collaboration and sharing of experience save people from reinventing wheels. I am grateful to all those colleagues who have permitted me to report what they have achieved. Once you have read this book I hope that you will seek out some of these pioneers and hear about their experience first-hand.

Competences do not provide a 'quick fix' for the school with management problems. They offer an approach which can help teachers to tackle such problems honestly and constructively with the aim of developing an effective self-managing school. They can also help the good school to be even better!

Derek Esp
November 1992

Part One

Introducing Competences

Chapter 1

Are You Competent?

Introduction

Are you a competent manager? Can you prove it to your colleagues in school, your immediate boss, the governors or yourself? An increasing number of teachers with management responsibilities are using competence-based schemes to further their professional development in a systematic way. Some school governing bodies are also piloting the use of assessment centres to help them to select headteachers. They are aware of the inadequacies of existing selection interviews and see attractions in the use of a more 'scientific' assessment.

This book is not written by a competence 'guru' for researchers. It is aimed at school managers at all levels, including those primary, secondary or special school teachers who are thinking of moving into a job where they will have to manage the work of their colleagues. My aim is to provide you with some examples of what is happening already and to report the views of teachers who have already used a competence model to aid their own professional development. Some wider issues are also discussed, not least the need for a national strategy for competence-based management development in schools. Finally, having read all about it, you are invited to consider the potential benefits for your own professional growth. If you really become enthusiastic, you might suggest that other colleagues in school give competences a try as well. A growing number of teachers find competences helpful for reviewing and improving the quality of individual, team or whole school management practice. But, competence-based approaches are only worth pursuing if they help to improve the effectiveness of teaching and pupil learning in schools.

The use of competence models in management development is not new. For example, in 1983 Cadbury Schweppes defined the success criteria for the use of competences as follows:

- each manager should be able to define his or her job in competence terms and pursue improvements in personal competence by setting learning objectives at least annually;
- every newly appointed person should commence work with agreed development objectives;
- challenges, pressures and major change should be described in competence terms;
- the organization should be aware of and make optimum use of the strengths which it has available at any one time; people/job mismatches should be brought to the surface and addressed; and
- more imagination should be introduced into the rotation of managers.

These long-term goals have enjoyed top management support over time and at key stages (Glaze 1989). This is one example where the use of a competence-based approach has been an important part of a strategy to achieve effective management development. Can competences help schools to achieve similar success?

It is easy to be sceptical about the competence movement. At present it promises to become another bandwagon. I was advised early in my career that bandwagons are like buses, ie there will be another one along any minute. Reciting impressive lists of competences does not produce them in the individual manager by spontaneous combustion. The competence movement tries to do better than that. The competences required of managers are defined and methods of developing each competence are identified. It is readily recognized that some competences cannot be improved significantly by training or development activities.

Even so, the critics of competency approaches are cautious about fragmenting the individual manager. Management is more than the sum of a bundle of discrete competences.

The case for increased competence

In his annual report for 1990 the Senior Chief Inspector (SCI 1990) reported that the management of schools left much to be desired. In only about a third of those inspected was senior management considered to be particularly effective. The School Management Task Force outlined the many new demands on schools in the Preface to their 1990 Report and went on to spell out the disillusionment and exhaustion that would follow if policy makers did not consider the impact of so many changes on school management. Further changes are proposed in the Parent's Charter (DES 1991) and the 1992 White Paper (DES 1992). It is clear that natural flair and panache will be insufficient to create and maintain a high quality of management in schools.

I am not convinced that policy makers have understood the real impact of all these changes on school management. The weakening of the role of the local education authority (LEA) and the increase in the number of self-managed schools will require competent self-management. Schools will be providing learning opportunities without access to a unified, comprehensive support structure. Like the 'learning company' the school will need to be 'an organization which facilitates the learning of all its members and continuously transforms itself' (Pedlar, Boydell and Burgoyne 1989).

If your school is to behave like a learning company it will be necessary for you to be clear of your place in the achievement of your school's effectiveness. You will also need to gain the skills of auditing your own performance and that of others engaged in school management. It will be a key requirement for each school to recruit, develop and nurture effective managers of high calibre in order to serve pupils and the community well against the background of increased national expectations and the regular cycle of national inspections.

Understanding competence – some underlying problems

One of the key contributors to the competence movement in the United Kingdom (Burgoyne 1989) has recognized a fundamental problem. His own definition of competence sounds reasonable. It is 'the ability and willingness to perform a task'. Yet, he observes that management usually has to create and define its own task. Competence is an attractive concept for managers however because it concerns action and not only possession of knowledge. Burgoyne has identified eight underlying problems that have to be addressed before a move can be made from a straightforward concept of managerial competence to assessment or professional development based on competences.

- Management is not the sequential exercise of discrete competences. Competence lists illuminate facets of a complex whole. How do we reintegrate competence ratings to achieve a view of holistic managerial performance?
- There is no technical approach to measurement of competence. Assessment can only be by way of grounded and informed judgement.
- There is the problem of universality. All managerial jobs are different at the detailed level but the same at a high level of abstraction. It may be possible to identify underpinning competences such as basic literacy and numeracy, basic analytical and decision making skills and basic financial awareness and knowledge about information technology. There are also overarching competences such as being able to learn, change, adapt, forecast, anticipate and create change. These are the meta-competences that underpin effective action in particular situations.
- The moral, ethical, political and ideological aspects of management have to be addressed. Values and mission are very much a part of management. Competent management has to involve engaging and mutually adjusting individual and organizational values.
- The very nature of management is a problem. It is a creative activity which moves its boundary.
- There are many 'right' ways to manage and any competence-based system must allow for this.
- Being competent is different from having competences. Managerial competences cannot just be used as a tool-kit list. 'The necessity of developing the whole person cannot be driven out of any effective approach to management development'.
- The issue of collective competence has to be addressed. People work in teams and groups where goodwill and co-operation are required. It is important to develop collective competences.

These issues have to be considered carefully. They cannot be solved by an individual manager or school wishing to develop their own competence model. They do offer the basis for a careful examination of the models on offer and may prevent school managers from leaping into crude DIY schemes that may, in the end, diminish rather than enhance the improvement of individual and team managerial competence.

The origins of competence-based education and training

Developments in the United States of America

The origins of this approach go back to the 1920s in the USA. By the 1960s there was an attempt to develop competences for teacher education. In 1968 the United States Office of Education funded eight pilot programmes for initial teacher education. The project guidelines sought to achieve a precise specification of competences or behaviours to be learned by trainee teachers. The modularization of instruction was also recommended. Plans were made for evaluation, feedback and field experience. It was hoped that this new approach would apply across the board in higher education. At that time there was considerable resistance from teachers in higher education not least because of the wholesale revision of programmes that would be required.

During the late 1970s there was a move to develop management competences for managers in industry and commerce based upon the distinguishing characteristics of managers who demonstrate superior performance at work. As a result of this movement there were attempts to develop competences for school principals. One such example was the initiative taken by the National Association for Secondary School Principals (NASSP). It established a set of generic competences for school principals for use in assessment centres. These centres provide information for selection and development purposes. The NASSP approach has extended to Australia, Canada, the Netherlands, Sweden and the United Kingdom.

Because of the hiccup in the late 1960s competence approaches in the USA moved into education as a result of developments elsewhere. The US Government supported the development of competencies but did not attempt to create a national set of standards or requirements.

Developments in the United Kingdom

The work done in the USA was modified and developed in the United Kingdom. Research in British universities had been limited. Before the British government took a major initiative in this field, some major companies had developed the use of competence approaches based on the work done in the USA.

The United Kingdom Government has sought to develop a national strategy for vocational qualifications. The National Council for Vocational Qualifications (NCVQ) was set up to 'secure standards of occupational competence and ensure that vocational qualifications are based on this'. In the 1988 White Paper (Department of Employment 1988) one of the six principles for the new training and enterprise framework was outlined as: 'there must be recognized standards of competence, relevant to employment, drawn up by industry led organizations covering every sector and every occupational group, and validated nationally'. The development of National Vocational Qualifications (NVQs) and the work of the Management Charter Initiative (MCI) to develop generic Occupational Standards for Managers are taking place within this framework. The national effort has given considerable impetus to the development of competence-based qualifications. The management standards have been used by teachers in some of the projects described in this book.

Competences – two major movements?

In the USA the work initiated to identify the competences of superior performers was based on the qualities, skills and behaviours of effective managers. In the UK the NVQ framework has put the emphasis on outcomes in terms of the performance required for a manager to perform at an average level of performance.

Much research has concentrated upon the characteristics linked to superior performance. This approach is described in Chapter Two which also provides some examples from British industry. The work on generic management standards in the UK has attempted to cover all competences including the basic knowledge and skills required for average managerial performance. The work done so far has mainly used functional analysis which has identified the manager's basic duties and tasks. This approach is described in Chapter Three.

In practice, it is possible to find many initiatives which mix and match the competences of superior performers together with competences at the level of the basic skills and knowledge required by all managers. Process (how managers go about their task) and outcomes (what they are expected to achieve) both have their place. The options and permutations suitable for the development of school managers are discussed in Chapter Ten.

Using competence-based management development in school

This book provides only a brief introduction to the complexities of competence models, and there are examples of how these models have been used to assist management development in schools. Some schemes draw upon American research into the characteristics of superior performers. Others use the generic management standards developed in the UK or have adapted them for school use.

The projects described in later chapters have been chosen as illustrations of the work which is taking place in schools. There are other successful initiatives which are not described in this book in any detail but which are building up valuable experience of competences. For example, the Cheshire LEA is about to test its Cheshire Education Management Programme (CEMP) in schools. This, with its competence model, was originally developed for colleges of further education. At the time of writing more local education authorities (LEAs) and schools are joining one of the established assessment centre or management development programmes or are developing their own model. The projects described are not meant to represent the 'best buys'. They are examples of the variety of current initiatives and provide helpful insights into the possible applications of a competence-based approach to individual, team and whole school management development.

The practical uses of competences and the support required by individuals and schools are considered in Chapters Ten and Eleven.

The language of competence

There are spelling variations that may provide a clue to the origin of a competence/y model. The American-based models speak of competency and competencies. The UK variation is competence and competences. In one way the spelling may provide a clue to the pedigree of a model! In this book, I use the UK spelling.

Each scheme has to be considered in the light of its own definition of competence or competency. The schemes which draw upon the study of superior performers are likely to prefer this kind of definition: 'An underlying characteristic causally linked to superior performance on the job' or 'an underlying characteristic in that it may be a motive, trait, skill, aspect of one's own self image or social role or a body of knowledge used by an individual' (Boyatzis 1982). In the UK competence has been defined as 'a description of something which a person who works in a given occupational area should be able to do. It is a description of an action, behaviour or outcome which the person should be able to demonstrate' (Training Agency 1988). Another UK definition is 'the ability to perform work activities to the standards required in employment'. (NCVQ 1988). Burgoyne's definition includes reference to motivation: 'Competence is the ability and willingness to perform a task. This can encompass knowledge, skill, understanding and will'. (Burgoyne 1989). Another helpful definition is 'being able to perform whole work roles, not just specific skills and tasks, to standards expected in employment, in real working environments. Work roles are not a bundle of tasks or routine procedures'.

The perfect definition is elusive. One thing is certain however. The use of competence-based development programmes focuses on the workplace where competence is best demonstrated and validated. For this reason, like marriage, such programmes should not be 'taken in hand unadvisedly, lightly or wantonly' (Church of England 1662). This particular bandwagon will be capable of rolling right into the head's office to change management style, expectations and performance. The potential gains are considerable but individuals, teams and schools have to be prepared to make real changes. In all of the examples described, teachers speak of the need to talk honestly to each other and to have the will to make improvements.

A checklist

I hope that you have been encouraged to read on. Some of the questions you need to ask are:

- Where does the scheme come from? Is the competence model based on the characteristics of superior performers; on functional analysis of the requirements for average performance? Or is it a hybrid?
- What is the definition of competence/competency used in the scheme?
- Is the model user friendly? Is the language understandable or does it require interpretation for use in school?
- Where and how has the scheme been tested?
- For what purposes have teachers used the model?
- Is there evidence of positive feedback from users? Is their verdict based on sound evidence?
- Are there any ways in which I might use a competence model in my own professional development or as a means of developing my team or my school?

Now to repeat a non-governmental health warning. Competence-based management development requires honesty with your colleagues and a willingness to change your management practice or modify your management style. This book can help you to consider the challenge and the opportunities for improvement before you decide to take some action for your own development or that of your school.

If you decide to go ahead this book should help you to identify possible sources of help, not least those teachers who have already used competence-based approaches for their own development as managers.

References

Burgoyne, J., 'Opinion', in *Transition*, February 1989.

Boyatzis, R. E., *The Competent Manager: a Model for Effective Performance* (Chichester: John Wiley and Sons, 1982).

Church of England, 'The Form of Solemnization of Marriage', *The Book of Common Prayer* (various publishers, 1662 onwards).

Department of Employment, *Employment in the 1990s* (London: HMSO, 1988).

Department of Education and Science *Choice and Diversity: a New Framework for Schools*, White Paper Cm 2021 (London: HMSO, 1992).

Department of Education and Science, Senior Chief Inspector, Annual Report 1990, (London: HMSO, 1991).

Department of Education and Science, *The Parent's Charter: You and Your Child's Education*, (London: HMSO, 1991).

Department of Education and Science, School Management Task Force, *Developing School Management: The Way Forward* (London: HMSO, 1990).

Glaze, Tony, 'Cadbury's Dictionary of Competence', in *Personnel Management*, July 1989.

NCVQ, *The NVQ Criteria and Related Guidance*, (1988).

Pedlar, M., T. Boydell and J. Burgoyne, 'Towards the Learning Company', in *Management Development and Education* Vol.20/1, 1989.

Training Agency, *Guidance Note 3*, (1988).

Chapter 2

Identifying the Characteristics of Superior Performers

What is superior performance?

A review of research into leadership effectiveness may help to provide a background to this Chapter. The characteristics of effective leadership and effective management are taken to be synonymous when looking at the characteristics of superior performers.

Leadership effectiveness is usually defined by criteria such as subordinate commitment to task objectives, subordinate satisfaction with the leader, and the success of the leader's group or organization in performing its mission and attaining its objectives.

There are several approaches to the study of leadership:

- The personal qualities of leaders are examined and an attempt is made to identify the traits and skills that contribute to the leadership success.
- The 'power influence' approach attempts to explain leadership effectiveness differently, ie in terms of the source and amount of leader power and the manner in which it is exercised.
- The 'behaviour approach' seeks to identify the pattern of behaviours and activities that are characteristic of effective leaders.
- Situational theories cut across these three approaches and emphasize how aspects of the leadership situation determine what traits, forms of influence or patterns of behaviour are essential for leadership effectiveness (Yukl 1981).

Figure 2.1 *Competences and performance*

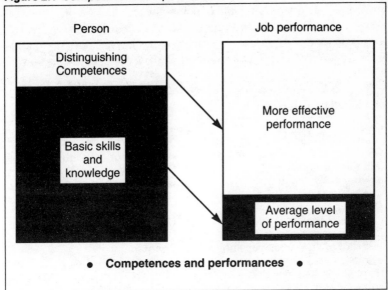

In work undertaken in the USA up to the early 1980s a number of traits were found which were beneficial to managerial effectiveness. These were self confidence; a need for socialized power; need for achievement; desire to compete with peers; respect for authority figures; tolerance for high stress; high energy level; interest in oral, persuasive activities; and relevant technical, conceptual and interpersonal skills. It must be remembered that this work was undertaken in the context of American business management.

Competence models

I am grateful to Bertie Everard for his description of the competence approach which developed in the USA in the late 1970s (Everard 1990). The following description is derived from his article. The American Management Association (AMA) joined with McBer Corporation, a consultancy firm, to answer the question: 'what are the distinguishing characteristics of managers who display superior performance in organizations?' In the research project a sample of 2,000 managers in 41 occupational categories within 12 private and public sector organizations was used to identify superior, average and poor performers. In identifying those competences that supplement the basic skills and knowledge required to do the job to an average level of performance the Americans identified some key clusters of competence. Figure 2.1, from Everard's article, provides an illustration of this.

The four key clusters of competence identified in the AMA work are shown in the box below:

Clusters	Competences
Goal and management action (This deals with a manager's initiative, image, problem solving skills and goal orientation.)	1. Efficiency orientation 2. Proactivity 3. Concern with impact 4. Diagnostic use of concepts
Directing subordinates (This involves a manager's freedom of expression both in terms of giving directives and orders as well as giving feedback to help develop subordinates.)	1. Use of unilateral power 2. Developing others 3. Spontaneity
Human resource management (Managers with these competences have positive expectations about others, have realistic views of themselves, build networks or coalitions with others to accomplish tasks and stimulate co-operation and pride in work groups.)	1. Accurate self-assessment 2. Self control 3. Stamina and adaptability 4. Perceptual objectivity 5. Positive regard 6. Managing group process 7. Use of socialized power
Leadership (A manager's ability to discern the key issues, patterns or objectives in an organization, and then conduct himself or herself and communicate in a strong fashion.)	1. Self confidence 2. Conceptualization 3. Logical thought 4. Use of oral presentations

Application of the AMA/McBer Competence Model

Assessing competence

Everard provides a useful summary of the application of the model in assessment centres. He describes the procedure followed:

1. An assessor interviews each manager about critical incidents and codes the responses against the competence model.
2. A group of managers are put into various simulations of the 'real world'.
3. A behavioural feedback form is completed by the manager's peers.
4. A workplace questionnaire mirroring the competence model is completed by colleagues and by the manager.
5. A battery of psychological tests and other instruments are used, as well as a management style questionnaire.
6. The manager does a self description exercise. Skilled assessors then interpret all this information and give each manager feedback.

Examples of assessment centres used in education are provided in Chapter Four (Educational Assessment Centre, Oxford) and Chapter Five (University of East London).

Developing competence

Everard also provides an example of what might take place in a typical competence development workshop. A group of managers are brought together to develop their competence in a six stage process:

1. Recognition of the competence when one sees it.
2. Understanding how it relates to management performance.
3. Assessment of performance in doing simulated tasks.
4. Experimentation – trying new behaviours.
5. Practice – using the competence on the job.
6. Application – consistent use.

Examples of applications of the American research in the UK

Some major British companies have used the model of 'soft skills' developed by the McBer Corporation and incorporated into the AMA programme. Use of this model predated the more recent MCI developments and may explain why a number of enterprises who have used competences for selection and development purposes have been slow to support the development of generic management standards. Some companies believe that organizations which develop their own competence research benefit from real 'ownership' of the results and commitment to the scheme. Competences developed this way are often context dependent and are shaped by means of synthesis from behavioural indicators.

The work of the McBer Corporation is said to be strong on 'excellence'. Competences are broken down into atomistic parts, most of them predispositions, but some of them are processes, eg 'developing others'. This not the place to go into all of the 'theological' arguments that arise when people compare the 'pure' McBer approach, variations of it or later developments.

The following examples show how some companies have developed competence models contextualized for the needs of their organisation.

Cadbury Schweppes

This account is based upon an article written by Tony Glaze (Glaze 1989). Cadbury Schweppes use a variety of instruments for management development, including competences. Competence data is considered to have more value than the other approaches when making decisions about individual development.

From long experience the company has concluded that different groups of competences need different treatment for developmental purposes. 'Several important competences, including initiative, creativity, risk taking and judgement, are unlikely to improve sufficiently to justify any sustained development activity' (Glaze). The Cadbury Schweppes dimensions of management competence are shown in the box below:

Dimensions of Management

Strategy Vision, critical thinking, innovation, environmental awareness, business sense.

Drive Self motivation, initiative, tenacity, energy, independence, risk taking, resilience.

Relationships Sociability, impact, acceptibility, awareness.

Persuasion Oral communication, written communication, flexibility, negotiation.

Leadership Delegation, subordinates' development.

Followership Followership, teamwork.

Analysis Problem analysis, numerical analysis, listening, creativity, judgement, intuition.

Implementation Planning and organizing, decisiveness,

> organization sensitivity, management control, work standards, detail handling, compliance, stress tolerance, adaptability, commitment.
> *Personal Factors* Integrity, management identification, career ambition, learning ability, technical/professional.

British Petroleum

This description of the BP use of competences is taken from an article by Greatrex and Phillips (Greatrex and Phillips 1989).

For some years BP has used residential assessment boards which 'filter' managers into a system for 'high flyers'. The approach to competences was described as follows: 'we have attempted to be situationally specific and to reflect the organization culture, especially in terms of its language, and not to rely on a general list of competences'.

The BP model is a mixture of concrete behaviours and sets of values and beliefs that match the BP culture. The model is shown in the box below:

The BP Competence Models

Eleven competences are grouped into four clusters.

Cluster	Competence
Achievement orientation	Personal drive
	Organizational drive
	Impact
	Communication
People orientation	Awareness of others
	Team management
	Persuasiveness
Judgement	Analytical power
	Strategic thinking
	Commercial judgement
Situational flexibility	Adaptive orientation

BP recognize that these competences look like other classification systems. They maintain that there is one fundamental difference: 'the behaviours listed within the clusters are expressed in terms of the language of the organization'.

The BP assessment boards provide feedback to individuals. The implications of assessment for training, personal development and overall career development are considered. There is a strong focus on self-development.

National Westminster Bank – using Schroder's High Performance Management Competences

This description is based upon an article written by Dr Tony Cockerill (Cockerill 1989).

In recent years Schroder has developed a model which tries to take account of the needs of modern enterprises in a context of high technology and rapid change (Schroder 1989). The National Westminster Bank provide an example of the use of this model.

Work began in 1985 to search for a competence model that would assist a rapidly changing institution. A four year study of all worldwide competence models available was undertaken by a seconded member of staff at the London Business School (Cockerill 1989). It was concluded that Schroder's model provided the basis for development. Work was done on Schroder's eleven high performance managerial competences which would 'raise performance beyond adequacy to excellence'. The research concluded that many of the 'soft' skills sought could be used and identified in simulated assessment.

Cockerill summarized the achievements of the study as follows:

'... our work at NatWest has enabled us to identify high performance managerial competences, relevant to rapidly changing environments and flexible forms of organization, which can be reliably measured...and significantly related to measures of performance now used as the basis for development' (Cockerill).

NatWest use self report inventories and assessment centres to develop the dynamic aspects of management. The approach is used to build on people's strengths and to assist the employer to build complementary teams. The high performance managerial competences are shown in the box on the following page.

Schroder's Eleven High Performance Managerial Competences

Information search Gathers many different kinds of information and uses a wide variety of sources to build a rich informational environment in preparation for decision making in the organization.

Concept formation Builds frameworks or models or forms concepts, hypotheses or ideas on the basis of information; becomes aware of patterns, trends and cause/effect relations by linking disparate information.

Conceptual flexibility Identifies feasible alternatives or multiple options in planning and decision making; holds different options in focus simultaneously and evaluates their pros and cons.

Interpersonal search Uses open and probing questions, summaries, paraphrasing, etc to understand the ideas, concepts and feelings of another; can comprehend events, issues, problems, opportunities from the viewpoint of another person.

Managing interaction Involves others and is able to build cooperative teams in which group members feel valued and empowered and have shared goals.

Developmental orientation Creates a positive climate in which individuals increase the accuracy of their awareness of their own strengths and limitations and provides coaching, training and developmental resources to improve performance.

Impact Uses a variety of methods (eg persuasive arguments, modelling behaviour, inventing symbols, forming alliances and appealing to the interest of others) to gain support for ideas, strategies and values.

Self confidence States own 'stand' or position on issues; unhesitatingly takes decisions when required and commits self and others accordingly; expresses confidence in the future success of the actions to be taken.

Presentation Presents ideas clearly, with ease and interest so that the other person (or audience) understands what is being communicated; uses technical, symbolic, non-verbal and visual aids effectively.

Proactive orientation Structures the task for the team; implements plans and ideas; takes responsibility for all aspects of the situation.

Achievement orientation Possesses high internal work standards and sets ambitious yet attainable goals; wants to do things better, to improve, to be more effective and efficient; measures progress against targets.

Conclusion

You will realize that the development of a competence model involves a considerable amount of groundwork. The organizations concerned spent considerable time analysing their present and future requirements, developing a detailed competence model and devising appropriate instruments for helping managers to develop particular competences. In each example the scheme was designed to reflect the values, management style and operational requirements of the company.

Some of the work undertaken in schools has been based on the American research. Examples are provided in Chapter Four and Chapter Five.

References

Cockerill, A. P., 'The Kind of Competence for Rapid Change' *Personnel Management*, the monthly magazine of the Institute of Personnel Management, September 1989.

Cockerill, A. P., 'Managerial Performance as a Determinant of Organisational Performance'. Doctoral Research at the London Business School 1989.

Everard, Bertie, 'The Competency Approach to Management Development', in *Management in Education*, Vol.4/2, Summer 1990.

Glaze, Tony, 'Cadbury's Dictionary of Competence' in *Personnel Management*, the monthly magazine of the Institute of Personnel Management, July 1989.

Greatrex, Julian, and Peter Phillips 'Oiling the Wheels of Competence', in *Personnel Management*, August 1989.

Schroder, H. M., *Managerial Competence: the Key to Excellence* (Iowa Kendall/Hunt, 1989).

Yukl, G., *Leadership in Organisations*, Englewood Cliffs, NJ: Prentice Hall, 1981).

Chapter 3

The Development of Occupational Standards for Managers*

The National Forum for Management Education and Development have developed generic management standards through their executive arm, the Management Charter Initiative (MCI). The standards are intended to be transferable so that, for example, a manager attaining accreditation of competence as a manager in a school will automatically meet the requirements for a manager in any other occupation at the same level.

Management qualifications framework

	Management Standards	S/NVQ Level	Awarding Body
	Senior Management Standards		Standards under development
M2	Middle Management Standards	S/NVQ 5	BTEC, HMC, IIM
M1	First Line Management Standards	S/NVQ 4	BPICS, BTEC, HMC, IIM, ISM, NEBSM, RSA, SCOTVEC
M1S	Supervisory Management Standards	S/NVQ 3	BTEC, ISM, NEBSM, RSA, SCOTVEC

These Management Standards are based upon the performance of an individual in an occupational role. They represent good practice and not minimum requirements. They do not attempt to categorize managers in terms of performance against the characteristics of superior performers. Managers are either 'competent' or 'not yet competent' and there is no attempt to create a norm referenced

---

*This chapter draws on various MCI publications.

heirarchy of competence as is the case with models used for assessment of staff for promotion.

The development of the MCI Standards

Functional analysis was used to develop the Standards at levels I and II. It may be helpful to look at the MCI's own guidelines for the use of MI Standards in more detail as an example of the MCI approach.

Management I (MI) Standards are for 'first line managers'. The MCI has provided guidance on the use of these standards (MCI 1991). The MI Standards form the basis of a National Vocational Qualification (NVQ) level 4. A range of applications for the standards are encouraged however which need not involve accreditation. 'They can be used as a valuable blueprint for:

- designing job specifications;
- developing learning and development programmes;
- identifying skill requirements and development needs;
- appraisal systems;
- assessing daily activities to sharpen performance and as a means of setting individual standards and performance levels to underpin existing quality initiatives such as BS5750 and Total Quality Management.'

Who are the first line managers?

The definition of 'first line manager' is clearly described in the MI guidelines. The first level of management is seen as the key to the operation of any organization and can be occupied by a variety of individuals. These may be experienced staff who have progressed through the supervisory ranks, recent entrants to an organization in the early stages of their careers, people returning to employment after a career break or specialists who have a significant managerial component to their job. Whilst job titles and accountabilities may vary there are many common features in the roles they undertake. All will be responsible for the direction and control of the activities of other people, achievement of results and the efficient and effective use of resources provided to them. First line managers are seen as people required to be proactive within the narrow focus of the function or area for which they are responsible but reactive in terms of the general direction of the organization. As well as dividing up and managing the flow of work, setting performance targets, developing their staff, providing instructions, monitoring and controlling progress against the objectives set for them, there is likely to be a good deal of negotiating and discussing with colleagues as well as giving feedback to their senior managers.

The First Line MCI Management Standards (M1)

The research undertaken to define the management standards for first line managers led to a decision to group the functions they undertake into four specific areas – management of operations, resources, people and information. However, the MCI Standards recognize that the scope and complexity of the activities undertaken by first line managers is fairly limited, working within tight constraints and with limited freedom of action. The standards are seen by MCI to represent what most managers should be able to achieve in the first level of management.

The nature and format of the management standards is:

Units of competence Each unit describes in broad terms what is expected of a competent manager in particular aspects of the job.

Elements of competence Each unit consists of a number of elements of competence. These reflect the skills, knowledge and abilities that first line managers are expected to possess. The elements are the basis of assessment of competence in this scheme.

Performance criteria Each element is described by performance criteria which specify the outcomes which a manager has to achieve in order to demonstrate competent performance. These are the basis upon which evidence of competence is judged by the assessor.

Range indicators For each element there is a set of range indicators which describe the range of instances and situations in which an element is applied.

Evidence requirements Each element has a detailed evidence specification outlining the amount and coverage of evidence required to ensure that competent performance is achieved.

The Occupational Standards for Management I are shown in Figures 3.1 and 3.2.

Figure 3.1 *Occupational standards for managers*

Occupational Standards for Managers (Management I) *Key Purpose: To Achieve the Organisation's Objectives and Continuously Improve its Performance*		
Key Roles and their associated Units of Competence		
Key Role	*Manage Operations*	I 1 Maintain and improve service and product operations
		I 2 Contribute to the implementation of change in services, products and systems
Key Role	*Manage Finance*	I 3 Recommend, monitor and control the use of resources
Key Role	*Manage People*	I 4 Contribute to the recruitment and selection of personnel
		I 5 Develop teams, individuals and self to enhance performance
		I 6 Plan, allocate and evaluate work carried out by teams, individuals and self
		I 7 Create, maintain and enhance effective working relationships
Key Role	*Manage Information*	I 8 Seek, evaluate and organise information for action
		I 9 Exchange information to solve problems and make decisions

The personal competences model

At first glance the Management Standards (M1) are preoccupied with functions. It has to be seen however in relationship to a Personal Competences Model (MCI 1991) which, although it stands alone, is implicit within the standards in terms of *how* an outcome is achieved. The model focuses on the management part of the job rather than on

Figure 3.2 *Occupational standards for managers: elements of competence*

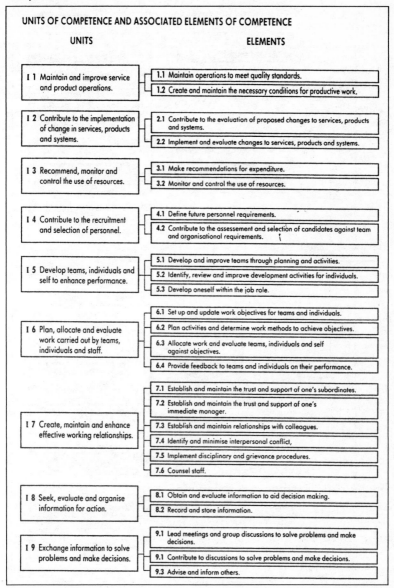

UNITS OF COMPETENCE AND ASSOCIATED ELEMENTS OF COMPETENCE

UNITS	ELEMENTS
I 1 Maintain and improve service and product operations.	1.1 Maintain operations to meet quality standards.
	1.2 Create and maintain the necessary conditions for productive work.
I 2 Contribute to the implementation of change in services, products and systems.	2.1 Contribute to the evaluation of proposed changes to services, products and systems.
	2.2 Implement and evaluate changes to services, products and systems.
I 3 Recommend, monitor and control the use of resources.	3.1 Make recommendations for expenditure.
	3.2 Monitor and control the use of resources.
I 4 Contribute to the recruitment and selection of personnel.	4.1 Define future personnel requirements.
	4.2 Contribute to the assessment and selection of candidates against team and organisational requirements.
I 5 Develop teams, individuals and self to enhance performance.	5.1 Develop and improve teams through planning and activities.
	5.2 Identify, review and improve development activities for individuals.
	5.3 Develop oneself within the job role.
I 6 Plan, allocate and evaluate work carried out by teams, individuals and staff.	6.1 Set up and update work objectives for teams and individuals.
	6.2 Plan activities and determine work methods to achieve objectives.
	6.3 Allocate work and evaluate teams, individuals and self against objectives.
	6.4 Provide feedback to teams and individuals on their performance.
I 7 Create, maintain and enhance effective working relationships.	7.1 Establish and maintain the trust and support of one's subordinates.
	7.2 Establish and maintain the trust and support of one's immediate manager.
	7.3 Establish and maintain relationships with colleagues.
	7.4 Identify and minimise interpersonal conflict,
	7.5 Implement disciplinary and grievance procedures.
	7.6 Counsel staff.
I 8 Seek, evaluate and organise information for action.	8.1 Obtain and evaluate information to aid decision making.
	8.2 Record and store information.
I 9 Exchange information to solve problems and make decisions.	9.1 Lead meetings and group discussions to solve problems and make decisions.
	9.1 Contribute to discussions to solve problems and make decisions.
	9.3 Advise and inform others.

Figure 3.3 *Personal competences model*

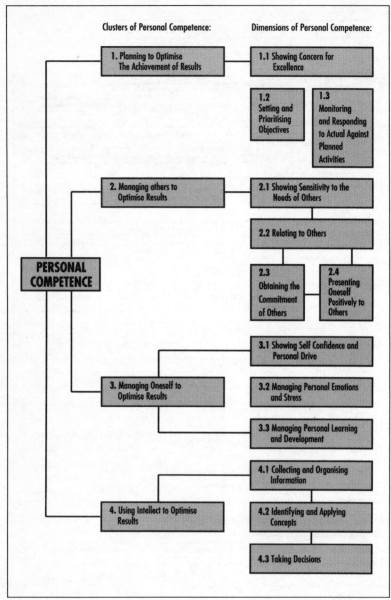

technical specialisms. The personal competence framework (see Figure 3.3) has four main clusters of personal competences concerned with getting results, managing others, managing self and using intellect. The Personal Competence Model links into Management I standards at Unit I.5 'Develop teams, individuals and self to enhance performance'. It is also to be found in the performance criteria of other elements.

Each cluster of personal competences has dimensions which are discrete sets of similar types of indicators. These indicators focus on behaviour so that managers can recognize how to demonstrate aspects of personal competence and develop their own competences which can then be learned, developed, observed and transferred to new situations. For example: 'demonstrates patience and tolerance when others are expressing themselves or encountering difficulties' is one indicator of the dimension 'showing sensitivity to the needs of others'. This model can be used as a template or as a diagnostic tool in its own right.

Specific uses of the personal competence model

The personal competence model has been used on its own in order to assist individuals and organizations:

- to define personnel specifications for recruitment (*nb* a personnel specification describes the personal characteristics sought in the job holder. It is used alongside a job description which describes the job to be done);
- to inform the appraisal process;
- as a training guide to help managers develop specific competences;
- as a framework to compare existing ways of managing with new expectations due to changes in organizational, technical or market requirements;
- to chart and inform the development of competence in being a team member or in developing teams;
- to design exercises to test and assess personal competences; and
- to inform managers in the assessment of the success of a particular project or initiative.

An example of the application of Dimension 3.1 'Showing self confidence and personal drive' demonstrates how the model can get to the heart of difficulties in the workplace. In this dimension the associated behaviours demonstrating the taking of initiative and responsibility include: 'Take control of situations and events (this includes actively trying to influence rather than passively accepting events, and pinning down others to their part in a course of action). Confront difficult issues openly'.

The personal competence model presents the human relations aspects behind a functional analysis model. It also encourages managers to tackle the people problems that so often sink well prepared development plans and well oiled administrative machines!

Knowledge and understanding

As well as providing the personal competences model the MCI have developed guidelines on the underpinning knowledge and understanding required by managers who wish to develop their competences (MCI 1992). Some young managers who are graduates with MBA qualifications will already have a good theoretical understanding of management theories and principles. A person promoted from the shop floor, or a teacher moving into school management from the 'chalk face' may need some help, possibly through self-study materials to develop their knowledge and understanding of management.

What is the first level of management in schools?

The MCI Standards define management strictly as the management of other adults. Educational definitions often include classroom management and management of pupils in other contexts too. Teachers using the MCI Standards have quickly observed however that management of classrooms and pupils in schools is management of operations, ie of the teaching and learning process which is the main activity of most first line managers in schools such as curriculum co-ordinators in primary schools and heads of department in secondary schools.

The use of MCI Standards in schools are described in Chapters Six and Seven. Chapter Eight describes the School Management South project. That research programme used functional analysis and adapted the MCI Standards in order to develop School Management Standards.

References

MCI (1992) *Management Standards Directory*, which consists of the following seven publications:

- Introducing Management Standards
- Middle Management Standards
- First Line Management Standards
- Supervising Management Standards
- Assessment Guidelines
- Personal Competence
- Developing a Portfolio

Part Two
Using Competences

Chapter 4

Using Competences — an American Model at Oxford

Background

The National Educational Assessment Centre (NEAC) project was started up by the Secondary Heads' Association and Oxford Polytechnic in 1990. Financial support also came from industry and government.

The main aim of the NEAC project is to improve preparation of individuals for headship by focusing on the assessment and development of key competences required for effective management and leadership in schools.

Assessment centres have been in use for over 50 years. They were used initially for selection purposes. They are also used to help inform the development of senior managers and those in leadership positions throughout the public and private sectors. The centre uses job related exercises designed to assess a number of key personal qualities or competences. The assessment centre process can provide an individual with a detailed diagnostic profile that can be used to target subsequent training and development. It can also be a complement to appraisal.

The NEAC assessment centres for development

During the pilot phase of the project (1990–92) just under one hundred participants from 25 local education authorities, the independent sector and the grant maintained schools have been through an assessment centre and will have received a diagnostic profile to inform the development of their management competences. The assessment centres have been located at various centres throughout the UK. Most participants have been deputy heads from secondary schools. The centres are adaptable for the requirements of senior staff in primary schools and in other education contexts.

The Educational Assessment Centre process

The centre is designed to contribute to the professional development of senior managers. The process itself has been devised and improved as the project has proceeded and there has been an external evaluation of the first stage of development.

There are four key components of the Educational Assessment Centre (EAC) process. These are:

- Identification of the management competences required for success as a head. The competence model, and its adaptation are considered later in the chapter. Twelve competences, derived from an analysis of the nature of headship, form the basis of the EAC process.
- Design of job-related exercises to assess the competences. In a typical developmental EAC these will include two in-trays, two leaderless group discussions, a fact-finding exercise and an interview. Each competence is usually assessed in several exercises. A vital component is the close interrelationship between the competences and the exercises.
- Assessment of performance. Performance on the job-related exercises is assessed by staff who undertake a four day training course. They are usually either experienced heads or educators who regularly work with heads. Careful selection and training of assessors is a key requirement, not least because successful heads and senior inspectors do not always have the very specific skills required of an assessor. During the EAC process the assessors work in teams of six assessing the performance of six participants as they undertake the exercises.

Each participant will be assessed by five of the six assessors on different exercises so that the final assessment across the 12 competences is balanced. In the final stages of an EAC each assessor writes a report on one of the participants. The report is a very full account of a participant's performance on the 12 competences and is supported by objective evidence. The report concludes with suggestions for further professional development based on this diagnostic profile and also upon the participant's own views about his/her development needs.

- Further professional development. Each participant has a debriefing interview based on the EAC report. At this stage the EAC evidence is viewed alongside the participant's own perceptions about their development needs so that a plan of action can be agreed.

    The initial focus for further professional development is on the things that the participant can do 'on the job' supplemented by the opportunity to spend some time alongside a senior colleague (the mentor) in another school. For a deputy head wanting to prepare for headship the programme of development would include working more regularly with their own head as well as spending time with a mentor.

In addition, the EAC project provides a portfolio of opportunities which have been analysed according to the 12 competences. Training of heads as assessors or mentors is also seen as another professional development opportunity provided by the project.

Mentoring is provided for a period of two to three years following the EAC. The diagnostic profile and report make suggestions for development, participants are assigned to a mentor, and the mentor – 'protégé' relationship provides a means of planning and promoting further professional development for the participant.

The Competences

The competences were developed initially in the USA. They were modified for the purpose of this pilot project. Because the NASSP materials are used under licence it was not possible to start with a complete review and rewrite of the competence model. The list of 12 competences chosen from a larger list, represents those which are most characteristic of the requirements of headship. They are also the competences which can be assessed in the assessment centre context. The competences used are characteristic of superior performers. For each competence participants are rated at, above or below the average. The competences are shown below:

Administrative competences

1. Problem analysis: ability to seek out relevant data and analyse information to determine the important elements of a problem situation; searching for information with a purpose.
2. Judgement: ability to reach logical conclusions and make high quality decisions based on available information; skill in identifying educational needs and setting priorities; ability to evaluate critically written communications.
3. Organizational ability: ability to plan, schedule and control the work of others; skill in using resources in an optimal fashion; ability to deal with a volume of paperwork and heavy demands on one's time.
4. Decisiveness: ability to recognize when a decision is required (disregarding the quality of the decision) and to act quickly.

Interpersonal competences

5. Leadership: ability to get others involved in solving problems; ability to recognize when a group requires direction, to interact with a group effectively and to guide them to the accomplishment of the task.
6. Sensitivity: ability to perceive the needs, concerns and personal problems of others; skill in resolving conflicts; tact in dealing with persons from different backgrounds; ability to deal effectively with people concerning emotional issues; knowing what information to communicate and to whom.
7. Stress tolerance: ability to perform under pressure and during opposition; the ability to think on one's feet.

Communicative competences

8. Oral communication: ability to make clear oral presentation of facts and ideas.
9. Written communication: ability to express ideas clearly in writing; to write appropriately for different audiences – students, teachers, parents, etc.

Personal breadth competences

10. Range of interest: ability to discuss a variety of subjects –

educational, political, current events, economic etc; desire to actively take part in events.

11. Personal motivation: need to achieve in all activities attempted; evidence that work is important to personal satisfaction; ability to be self evaluating.

12. Educational values: possession of a well-reasoned educational philosophy; receptiveness to new ideas and change.

Evaluation of the Educational Assessment Centre pilot phase

The report of the external evaluators (Esp and Young 1991) examined various aspects of the project.

The competence model

The evaluators were asked to look at the model in use and not to examine alternatives at this stage. The evaluation report stated that most of the competences were in common use and well validated. Two competences seemed to be unique to this project, ie 'Educational values' and 'Range of interests'. Of the 12 competences only 'Range of interests' seemed to lack face validity. 'The assumption that successful experience of headship will correlate with having a wide range of interests is not borne out in the case of some successful heads' (Esp and Young 1991).

Participants were also invited to comment on the competence model. It must be remembered that this was a small group, ie the 24 people who attended the first two centres. Their responses were used to develop and improve assessor training and assessment processes at subsequent centres. There was a mixed response to the competences and to the ratings given. Most people seemed to find the experience positive and much of the assessment valid to them. It was difficult for the evaluators to judge responses which arose from an experience of this kind. They recommended statistical research to identify how well competence ratings discriminate between those taking part and how accurately they predict follow up measures of job performance. The evaluators also recommended a further study of how these competences might relate to other competence models being piloted in schools.

The assessment centre simulation exercises

The job-related simulation exercises take place over two days. The participants experience two leaderless discussion groups, a fact-finding exercise, two in-tray exercises and an interview. The relationship between the 12 competences and the exercises are shown in the table below.

Matrix of competences against opportunities to assess them					
Management competences	**Job-related exercises**				
	Leaderless group discussions		Fact-finding	In-trays		Interviews
	I	II		I	II	
1. Problem analysis	X	X	X	X	X	
2. Judgement	X	X	X	X	X	
3. Organizational ability			X	X	X	
4. Decisiveness			X	X	X	
5. Leadership	X	X				
6. Sensitivity	X	X	X	X	X	
7. Stress tolerance			X			X
8. Oral communication	X	X	X			X
9. Written communication				X	X	
10. Range of interests						X
11. Personal motivation						X
12. Educational values	X	X		X	X	X

The content of the exercises is real in terms of the information that headteachers deal with in the course of their work. The evaluators recommended some changes to the interview and these have been implemented.

Assessment

The external evaluators considered the procedure to be highly effective. 'The meticulous building of judgements towards the final assessment is straightforward.' This assisted the aim of achieving a holistic view of the individual participant through consensus discussion. Two teams of six assessors each consider a group of six participants. The task of the course director is to insist on evidence to support ratings. The aim is to ensure consistent standards and objectivity.

The EAC experience is demanding for participants and assessors alike. In the words of the external evaluators '...as with the contribution of the pig and the hen to the traditional breakfast, the assessors and the participants made either a sacrifice or a contribution to the EAC. Whether participants or assessors made the "sacrifice" is yet to be resolved!' (Esp and Young 1991).

External evaluation of mentor training

The external evaluators encountered an enthusiastic and positive response from trainees. The suggestion of a code of practice for mentoring came from the trainees at these early training sessions. This idea was immediately adopted by the project staff and developed further with the help of mentors

After care and follow-up — the mentoring process

Mentor selection

By the end of 1991 over 60 experienced heads had been trained as mentors. These heads came from 25 local education authorities, and from independent and grant-maintained schools.

The quality and experience of mentors nominated by clients is crucial. There are guidelines for mentor selection which seem to have been effective. It is made clear in the guidelines that mentors must be prepared to undertake certain tasks of self-analysis and to be explicit about their current approaches to conducting professional relationships.

Mentor selection and training

Headteachers are selected for the mentor role. They receive two days of training which begins with a review of the EAC process itself. The purpose is to help mentors to appreciate the intensity and objectivity of their protégé's experience. The programme is then run largely experientially, drawing upon the perspectives and expectations of the various people involved in the EAC programme, ie the protégé, the protégé's headteacher, the mentor and the person who provides the link between the EAC and the client group, eg the local education authority.

The mentor is provided with a menu of models and skills. The project strategy has been to re-examine the skills which heads already deploy and match them with the needs of the protégé and the requirements of the mentor role. Substantial time is spent on case work using data from EAC participants' reports suitably anonymized. Some of this practice is analytical and some is rehearsal of typical mentor-protégé discussions. A code of practice for mentoring establishes broad protocols so that everyone concerned has matching expectations of procedures and behaviours. This particular mentoring scheme enables discussion of individual development and is not necessarily interwoven with the needs of the school which, in some instances, might conflict with that individual development.

Headteachers as mentors

The project team recognize that a head mentoring in his/her own school is likely to be too close to the outcomes to see the development of the protégé objectively. The head might also wish to coach the individual to behave in a way most apposite for the school. There are other, potentially more serious, problems where a head may have an interest in curbing the development of an ambitious deputy. This 'detached' model of mentoring is intended to help the protégé to identify the skills, experience and philosophy that will complement and extend their current competences. The aim is to prepare them for future headship, and not only to improve their performance in their current school.

The mentor/protégé relationship

Protégés are encouraged to play the active role, using the mentor as a resource. This underlines the importance of self-motivation. Again, the mentor cannot dictate what is happening in the protégé's school. Each protégé has to decide what is feasible under their particular circumstances. The mentor is expected to work with the protégé for a period of two to three years. If the relationship does not work then a change of mentor is encouraged.

The code of practice spells out that it is not the mentor's job to secure a headship for the protégé. The mentor is not to be asked to act as a referee or make other enquiries of a career nature for the protégé. To do so might upset the balance of the relationship which should leave the action and initiative with the protégé.

Is mentoring effective?

The project team have written their own review and critique of the mentoring scheme (Green, Holmes and Shaw 1991). They distinguish clearly between coaching and mentoring. Coaching implies regular contact, a hierarchical relationship, a focus on skills and competences in action, feedback on performance and accountability. Mentoring in this scheme is more of a partnership. There may well be target-setting but it will be related to the protégé's development, and not to the practical management challenges of the protégé's school. Mentoring will embrace a wide view of development and may take into consideration personal and private matters which are often excluded from professional development and appraisal discussions. The approach is holistic. The relationship is driven by the protégé and the mentor is essentially responsive. This sets this approach to mentoring aside from the counselling and coaching role adopted by most headteachers.

There has been genuine enthusiasm for the role of mentor and for the potential it has for adding a new dimension to the development of senior staff in schools. There are still difficulties however in defining the role of the mentor adequately as a discrete one. Directive behaviours are difficult to avoid when a mentor is faced with a protégé who has a weak profile across a number of EAC competences. There is also an understandable tension between the confidentiality of mentoring and the inquisitive desire to know more about 'what is going on' in the protégé's school. In practical terms it may be erroneous to assume that the interpersonal skills of mentoring are widely known and practised in schools.

Further developments

The project is maintaining a network for mentors which will enable them to continue to share experiences. An evaluation has yet to take place of the work of mentors in the field and of the reactions of the heads of protégés' schools and employers to the effectiveness of the mentoring process.

Further review of the competence model

The 12 EAC competences have been the subject of a review which has compared them with other models and with the latest review of the same model in the USA (Esp 1991). A revised list is being prepared. This will be in use from September 1992.

Four new competences will be built into future exercises as follows:

1. A cluster of behaviours to be integrated into existing competences and including creative problem solving, divergent thinking, entrepreneurship and risk taking.
2. Developmental awareness of:
   - Self: taking continuous action to improve personal capability;
   - Others: identifying and providing opportunities to improve the capabilities of other people;
   - Institution: receptiveness to new ideas from others; ability to generate new ideas; ability to perceive longer-term changes and to prepare effectively for them and evidence of implementation of change.
3. Pedagogic leadership: this contrasts with the existing 'leadership' competence which is task and team focused. It includes:
   - Understanding and experience of the processes and techniques of teaching and learning;
   - Ability to evaluate classroom performance in relation to teacher objectives and student outcomes; and
   - ability to work effectively with teachers and students to improve classroom performance.
4. Boundary management or extra-organizational awareness where the manager:
   - Has a knowledge of changing situations outside the school, including local and governmental pressures, and can identify potential organizational problems and opportunities associated with them;
   - Bases actions on an awareness of the impact and implication of these wider societal and governmental factors and
   - has experience of managing conflict in these areas.

The present list of 12 competences will not be extended. Instead it is hoped to end up with a revised list of eight main competence headings.

Review of the NASSP Competences in the USA

It is interesting to compare a review of the same competence model that was reported in 1990. The Oxford team were able to draw upon this research (Esp 1991).

The Center for Assessment of Administrative Performance undertook a study of assessment centres for school principals (Bolton 1990). An initial task was to review the literature concerning effective principals, tasks to be accomplished by principals and dimensions to be considered for assessment. Concurrently, the Center was involved in a review of the literature concerning criteria, standards, and procedures used in the evaluation of teachers. Field work followed in 1986 and 1987 and the outcome was a set of procedures that would allow the results of assessment centres to be used for diagnostic as well as selection purposes in the USA. From a list of 24 dimensions of competence the study came up with a revised short list of 12 dimensions which were identified as being appropriate and of priority for assessment. The revised shortlist of 12 dimensions of competence included new dimensions: 'Educational values' and 'Instructional leadership and supervision'. This matches the desire in the Oxford project to give greater prominence to educational values and pedagogic leadership.

Other developments

The core work of the project has been the use of the assessment centre experience and mentoring support to develop the competences of senior staff in secondary schools. The range of activities is now extending further:

EACs for primary school professional development

A seconded primary head has produced EAC exercises appropriate for use with primary school staff and a three day EAC model is being planned with the co-operation of existing clients. The process is likely to include five exercises; an in-tray, a leaderless discussion group, a fact-finding exercise, a values exercise and an interview.

EACs for selection: primary and secondary

There is growing interest in the use of assessment centres for selection. Selection centres have already been run for primary and secondary school headship appointments. The candidates complete four exercises within a day (an in-tray, a leaderless group discussion, a fact finding exercise and a values exercise). The assessors take one and a half days to complete the assessment process.

Middle manager development

The project team are seeking a commercial partner who will help develop the EAC personal competences approach for middle manager development in schools.

Workshops

Workshops which are offered to headteachers, deputies and chairs of governors. These include: values, vision and mission for school leaders; management and leadership in the context of rapid change and quality in education. Another development is a one day workshop which uses typical headteacher's in-tray material to develop several management competences.

Regionalization

A regional EAC has been established in Scotland with the help of Dumfries and Galloway Regional Council. A seconded head is adapting EAC materials for the Scottish context. Work continues with Strathclyde Regional Council and the intention is to involve other Scottish regions.

Discussions are continuing with the aim of establishing further regional EACs throughout the United Kingdom. The leading group, institution or organization will vary for each region.

These regional developments imply that the Oxford EAC will adopt a co-ordinating, licensing, quality control and development role in the future. Regional representatives might sit on a steering or management committee in the near future.

Educational values

The NEAC project has a Gulbenkian-funded programme which is developing training approaches for senior staff in schools in the area of educational values. This development was reported to the 1992 British Education Management and Administration (BEMAS) Conference (Green 1992).

Accreditation

The EAC is now used as a starting point for candidates participating in the Master of Business Administration (MBA) course at Leeds Polytechnic. Other forms of accreditation for the EAC experience are being explored.

Links with other schemes

The project steering group are intending to work together with other projects, including the MCI as they develop generic management standards for senior managers.

Conclusion

A full review of the pilot phase of the NEAC project is available from the Department of Employment (Green 1992).

The NEAC project has achieved rapid development and is working with a significant number of client groups. It now has links with about 50 local education authorities and is also working with independent and grant maintained schools. It works with clients in all parts of the UK. The EAC is relatively expensive in terms of assessor time and overall cost. This has to be seen in the context of the need for more effective forms of leadership development. The search for greater cost effectiveness, and a wider range of applications for the competence model form part of current developments. The project is now moving away from the original competence model although the project team think it was correct to begin with a ready made scheme. After using that and becoming thoroughly familiar with it, they now feel better prepared to develop their model further to meet the requirements of UK schools.

This they intend to do in co-operation with others who are using competence-based approaches in the private and public sectors, including education.

References

Bolton, D. L., *Recent Developments in Methodology for Administrator Assessment Centers*, (University of Washington, 1990).

Esp, D., and M. Young, *Stage 1 Evaluation Report*, to the Director of the NEAC, (July 1991).

Esp, D., *Management Competences*, report to the NEAC Director, October 1991.

Green, H., 'Leadership, Values and Site-Based Management' Paper to BEMAS Annual Conference 1992 at Bristol.

Green, H., 'The Use of an Assessment Centre Process, a Personal Competency Model and Mentoring for the Development of Headteachers' Report for TEED, Department of Employment, 1992.

Green, H., G. Holmes and M. Shaw, *Assessment and Mentoring for Headship*, (Oxford: School of Education, Oxford Polytechnic, 1991).

Chapter 5

Developing and Using Management Competences: the North West, Cleveland and East London

Introduction

The three examples in this chapter demonstrate how people have taken advice and then developed a 'bespoke' model for their own specific purposes using competences based upon the characteristics of superior performers.

The Consortium for Education Management Development in the north west developed a competence model for their profiling project. This is described in this chapter. (An associated development at Manchester Polytechnic using the MCI Standards is described in Chapter Seven.)

The Cleveland/ICI Heads' Group provide an example of good co-operation between schools and a major private sector enterprise over some 12 years.

The University of East London provides an example of another assessment centre project. In this case co-operation with a major firm of consultants, local education authorities and schools has led to the development of the competence model. The university has a nation-wide research project looking at school leadership which will also inform the further adaptation and development of their assessment centre.

The Consortium for Management Development Profiling Project

Introduction

This account is based upon the reports of the project team and evaluators notably Geoff Bowles and Tony Beck (Beck, in O'Connor 1991; Bowles 1992). This was one of the profiling consortia projects funded by the School Management Task Force. The aim was to establish a programme of development and training for senior and prospective managers in schools and colleges consisting of four elements which would provide a structured approach to the development of education management skills and which would take account of experience, theoretical understanding and specific training.

This project started at the beginning of the 1989–90 academic year and ended in July 1991. It was supported by the staff of Education Management North West. The consortium brought together four local education authorities and six higher education institutions in the region.

Identification of development needs

The needs of teachers at the beginning of their career, teachers with posts of responsibility, newly appointed senior managers and experienced senior managers were considered. From the expressed needs of these groups grew the idea of putting together a coherent, career long development programme which, if completed, would ensure that a teacher had an adequate practical and theoretical training before taking up a senior management post in a school, and that teachers in senior posts would be given opportunities for further development of their management skills.

A framework for long term professional development

The use of competences was set in the general framework of a long term professional development plan with four elements:

Element one: this would provide teachers with the opportunity to record the various management activities, experiences and courses they undertake, in an education management profile. They would be asked to review these activities and to reflect upon them, with help and advice from a 'critical friend'. At the end of the year there would be a full review of the teacher's management development with a senior member of staff.

Element two: encouraged the teacher to move towards a more formal study of management when they felt ready to do so. There would be an opportunity to attend a management development centre (MDC), which would give feedback about their individual management competences and advice about further training opportunities. It was hoped that this element would lead to an award at certificate or diploma level.

Element three: ensured that the teacher who was promoted to a senior management post had access to a thorough and comprehensive development programme provided jointly by the school and the local education authority.

Element four: was an attempt to meet the needs of heads and deputies who had been in post for some time and who needed a phase of reflection and reassessment of their individual management style. The programme would take place at intervals over two years and would involve action learning, visiting other organizations, discussions with colleagues and management teaching with teachers involved in other elements of the programme.

The project was evaluated by an external evaluation team.

One hundred and fifty one teachers from primary and secondary schools participated in Element One in 1989–90. Of these, 44 proceeded to Element Two in 1990–91. In the same year a second cohort of 68 teachers completed Element One.

The development of a management competences model

A competences model was developed for use in the MDC course which provided a bridge between Elements one and two. The project team addressed the following questions:

- How do we know that those completing the profile have a sufficient breadth of appropriate management competences?
- How can we ascertain levels of competence across a range of individuals in a variety of situations? and
- How can we help teachers identify gaps in their overall managerial competence and support their future development?

Visits and a major literature search were used to look at assessment centres and competence models. Consultations with local education authorities and possible 'consumers' helped to identify needs relating to management development which might be addressed in the MDC.

Identifying the competences

Several alternative competence models were examined and discussed with experienced people who had developed and used competence models. The pilot project review (Beck 1991) notes 'we do know that our final model is close to others devised from more sophisticated methods, and we were keen to demonstrate that the overall task of helping teachers identify their strengths and weaknesses could be achieved before embarking on more costly procedures'.

The final MDC model identified 11 competences with accompanying descriptors of behaviour and performance criteria. The development of these is described in the project review (see O'Connor, in CEMD 1991).

The following core competences were chosen for school management:

1. Vision
2. Persistence
3. Planning skill
4. Critical thinking
5. Stress tolerance
6. Leadership skills
7. Influence skill
8. Confident self-image
9. Interpersonal relationships
10. Empathy
11. Capacity for self-development.

The working party then prepared detailed descriptions of what was meant by the terms used for each competence, together with behavioural examples applicable to schools.

It was emphasized by the working party that it was important to adopt a holistic approach notwithstanding the analytical methodology. Verbal and non-verbal communication were considered to be central. Educational values also needed to be considered. An individual's underlying philosophy also had to be understood.

The Management Development Centre – responses to the competence model

The positive reactions of observers at the centre and participants are recorded in the project review (Hoy 1991 and Cotton 1991). In a questionnaire designed to elicit the reactions of the teachers to the MDC courses 98 per cent of respondents found the activities undertaken stimulating or interesting. Sixty four per cent found the course very useful in terms of their own professional development and a further 35 per cent found the course useful.

There were also benefits for the observers who without exception commented that the opportunity to observe teachers taking part in a series of activities and being required to consider and identify the management competences involved, had been a profitable one for them as experienced education managers. Many of them remarked on the development of their own understanding, and expressed the wish to take their own learning forward through additional experiences.

The final report indicated that 'Evaluation of the development centres by those who took part shows that they were given a very high rating as an intense but significant experience in terms of management development for the individual' (Bowles 1992).

Further developments

Further work is proceeding on the design of the development centre model, with modification of the original. The demands made upon potential users have to be manageable in terms of time commitment and cost. There are uncertainties about the future role of the local education authorities. The biggest problem is that of funding which hampered the development of the Consortium for Education Management Development (CEMD) four element programme throughout the life of the project.

Learning from industry – competence-based professional development in Cleveland

Background

The Cleveland Local Education Authority established the Cleveland/ICI Head Teachers' Group following a conference in 1978. The group meets six or seven times a year, with an ICI training manager, to consider matters of mutual interest about management. The head-teachers represent all sectors of education; primary, secondary and tertiary, and include members who have moved into other management roles in areas such as local management of schools, appraisal and the Technical and Vocational Education Initiative (TVEI).

The project described draws substantially upon the work of the group, including Carol Robinson, Advisory Head Teacher for Management and Appraisal in Cleveland. During the period 1990–92 the group focused its attention upon competences. ICI had applied a competence focus as part of their graduate selection process since 1985 and had for some years supported its use in personal review. The head teachers investigated the potential of the ICI model for selection of teachers and for the professional development of teachers in the context of teacher appraisal.

What is a competence?

The work of the group exemplifies the classical approach to defining management competences described in Chapter Nine. The group accepted the definition used by their ICI colleagues: 'the predisposition to behave in ways shown to be associated with the achievement of successful outcomes'. It was noted that in part of the graduate selection process, the selection team based their conclusions on the principle that past behaviour is a good indicator of future behaviour. In a behaviour event interview candidates are asked to describe their approach to some activity or incident in which they played a significant part, or a time in their lives when they needed to influence someone. Skilled interviewers are listening for evidence of the demonstration of competences through the behaviours described.

At an early stage in discussions the head teachers group looked at the ICI definition of a competence. They decided not to look at the competences used by ICI at this stage, but considered school management in the context of the competence definition only. A group of 16 middle managers was identified and interviewed by trained interviewers. The interviews were taped and transcribed. Four of the transcripts were considered initially. These outlined possible competence clusters. Ideas were pooled and a provisional list of 22 competences was identified. This draft list was then examined in the light of 12 more papers from group members. Only after that process was a list of 14 competences identified. These were grouped under four clusters: achieving; thinking; self and working with others.

Each identified competence was described by a brief 'essence' statement and by a set of behaviours which helped to show how the competence expressed itself in action.

The middle management competence framework was then devised. This is shown in the box below:

The Middle Management Competence Framework – a Summary

	Competence	Essence statement
Achieving cluster		
1.	INITIATIVE	Has energy and resourcefulness enabling one to act without prompting.
2.	CRITICAL INFORMATION SEEKING	Actively pursues the key information required to understand and/or progress an issue
3.	RESULTS ORIENTATION	Sets goals to exceed existing standards.
Thinking cluster		
4.	ANALYTICAL THINKING	Breaks things down into essential elements.
5.	CONCEPTUAL THINKING	Finds patterns, syntheses, builds up.
6.	FORWARD THINKING	Takes the long term into consideration.
Self cluster		
7.	POSITIVE SELF-AWARENESS	Belief in oneself.
8.	THOROUGHNESS	Concern for completeness and accuracy.
9.	PERSEVERANCE	Sustains effort over a long period to make progress.

Working with others cluster

10.	CONCERN WITH IMPACT	Takes action to have a desired effect by anticipating or responding to the feelings/ needs and concerns of others.
11.	INTERPERSONAL AWARENESS	Draws inferences about and maintains awareness of others' interests, moods and concerns.
12.	STRATEGIC INFLUENCING	Selects appropriate influencing strategy.
13.	ASSERTIVENESS (INDEPENDENCE)	Maintains own line in difficult situation.
14.	TRAINING AND SUPPORT NEEDS OF OTHERS	Takes action to support the development of others.

The group identified seven competences as critical. Statistical analysis of results had indicated a significant difference in the frequency of their occurrence where outstandingly successful management situations were compared with moderately successful management situations. The seven critical competences are:

Initiative
Analytical thinking
Positive self awareness
Concern with impact
Interpersonal awareness
Strategic influencing
Assertiveness.

These competences were considered to be useful in selection provided that interviewers were skilled in the area of behavioural event interviewing. For example, a person who demonstrated initiative could describe situations where they can be seen to take action without prompting, recognize an opportunity and take advantage of it, make proposals for change or improvement and make proposals to solve problems.

Application of this process for selection was seen as a long term development involving training of interviewers. The competences were seen to have more immediate application for professional development in the context of teacher appraisal. The competence based model would assist self-appraisal, classroom and task observation, and target setting between appraisers and appraisees. The group consider that, since competences are described as characteristic behaviours, they provide valid criteria for development. They also provide a common language and objectivity in discussion and planning for career development.

The headteachers went on to explore the possible application of the ICI model for personal development. In teacher appraisal it would be possible to follow the industrial model where:

- the individual, in dialogue with their manager, first identifies his or her objectives – 'What am I trying to achieve?, What final outcome am I looking for? What are my priorities?
- the next step is to identify the key tasks which must be undertaken to achieve the agreed objectives – 'What needs to be done to achieve this?'
- the third step is to identify the activities and behaviours which underpin the tasks and to relate these to the competences.

Since competences are described in terms of characteristic behaviours, the individual then has a model on which to base his or her personal development targets.

The head teachers group saw this process applying to self-appraisal, providing behaviour indicators for task observation and as an aid in the appraisal dialogue in order to determine development targets. Development targets can be discussed in terms of the steps described in the industrial model. It is then possible to consider the need for skills development, knowledge enhancement or change of context. This approach also provides a focus for the agreement of targets and the role of the appraisee, appraiser and school management in achieving those targets.

The group have now produced guidelines and proforma for use in the appraisal process for middle managers in the elements of self-appraisal, task observation and target setting. Having identified the areas where competence can be developed they are now seeking ways of implementing this approach. Some of their work in support of appraisal is mentioned in Chapter Ten.

For example, there is a process which provides feedback on how people actually use competences in their job compared with how they might ideally use them for most effective performance. The aim is to describe the actual and ideal profiles of a person's competences, to identify their strengths and weaknesses and to help them to make an assessment of their own development needs.

The group have also prepared a working document to provide guidance for individuals wishing to develop a competency. (Cleveland/ICI Head Teachers' Group 1992). This provides a list of behavioural indicators for each competence together with suggestions for self-development activities and ideas for the manager on how an individual's development might be supported. This support documentation is now being tested in schools.

The group is now looking at team building and will be considering the contribution of competences to that. They are also trying to make the materials more user friendly for schools. For example, school governors and heads may be uneasy about applying critical incident interviewing in a selection process. For this reason the group has now resolved 'to research, develop and refine the use of competences in the management of education in a way which continues the development of this group so that we have practical packages on competences to share with colleagues'.

The group has already prepared a booklet for colleagues in schools (Cleveland/ICI Head Teachers' Group 1992). It is designed for use by individuals. They can use it by themselves or together with their manager. The essential purpose is 'to help performance improvement through offering ideas, suggestions and learning experiences to aid the development of the fourteen competences'. The booklet works on the assumption that development is most often about releasing potential rather than changing people in any fundamental way, ie 'creating structured opportunities for people to improve progressively the capabilities they possess already'.

The group aim is to promote a more systematic and effective method of nurturing individual professional development through this competence-based approach.

Headteachers Assessment and Development Centre – University of East London

The description of this project draws extensively on the work of Geoff Lyons and Dilum Jirasinghe at the East London Business School at the University of East London. A full account of their work is outlined in a recent publication (Lyons and Jirasinghe 1992). The centre was designed and established in September 1991 in collaboration with occupation psychology consultants, Saville & Holdsworth Ltd.

The purpose of the assessment centre is to evaluate the skills and abilities of participants in 'a systematic, standardized and objective manner'. A centre may be residential or non-residential, either at the East London Business School premises or at premises provided by an LEA. An intensive one and a half day programme incorporates a range of work related assessment methods such as psychometric tests, simulations and interviews. These are intended to cover the head-teacher's current managerial skills and characteristics. It also involves a self-evaluation process. Participants receive feedback which includes a written profile summarizing individual managerial strengths and development needs. Agreement to this written profile is obtained through one-to-one feedback and the profile is then used as a basis for planning an individual management development programme.

The competence model

The initial work was undertaken with more than 60 headteachers, inspectors and education officers from all maintained schools sectors. In collaboration with a firm of management consultants, a rigorous job analysis was conducted. This looked at all current aspects of the headteacher's job. From this research a list of managerial criteria and competences has been derived. These criteria have been agreed by headteachers, inspectors and education officers involved in fieldwork stages as representing the current dimensions of the headteacher's job. The model is generally based on characteristics of superior performers, particularly the work of Boyatzis (1982).

Continuous updating of the dimensions is part of the methodology adopted. The researchers are currently conducting a national research project to ascertain whether or not phase/sector and gender differences amongst heads in terms of management competences exist.

The pilot assessment criteria are outlined in the box below. Please note that they are being amended and developed as the research progresses. They are not presented here in any rank order.

Pilot Assessment Criteria

Organizing/planning
Enjoys short and long term planning but is also able and willing to adapt plans to take account of change. Able to monitor and evaluate action plans, effectively delegating tasks and responsibility where appropriate. Is pro-active, seeks information and attends to appropriate level of detail. Makes effective/efficient use of available time.

Reasoning
Able to analyse and reason logically with complex oral and written information. Able to reason with moderately complex financial and marketing related information.

People orientation
Is socially confident, affiliative and able to build rapport in relationships. Analyses and understands the behaviour of others and is sympathetic and tolerant of them. Can relate the needs of individuals to wider organizational needs.

Influence
Is persuasive, diplomatic and is skilled in negotiating. Able to develop, use and maintain a network of contacts.

Communication
Can identify and use appropriate language and medium for presenting rational arguments:
In speech: clear, articulate and expressive, adapting style according to the audience and is skilled in listening, seeking and using confirmation and clarification to ensure understanding.
In writing: produces clear and grammatically correct written communication, eg proposals, papers, formal correspondence, memoranda and routine administration.

Job-related knowledge
Is aware of and understands rules, pertinent laws and procedures. Uses experiences to both learn and adapt and also keeps up-to-date on relevant issues.

Political awareness
Understands the power base and his/her role in relation to the wider organization/system. Is politically adept and aware of the importance of the political environment.

Decision making
Considers a range of options before making decisions. Is generally a democratic decision-maker – able and willing to take responsibility and will take decisions without consultation on a day-to-

---

day routine. Decisions are impartial, rational and based on objective data.

Leadership

Has a preference for leading and co-ordinating the team but will intervene and take control/direct the team when required. Involves team members in setting objectives. Motivates others, understands and assists in the development of staff.

Motivation/personal strengths/resilience

Displays commitment to the school and firmness of beliefs but is also able to switch off and take interest in a wider range of issues. Can deal positively with: conflicts of interest, harsh or unfair remarks and the pressures which can be created by demands for personal attention. Prefers to be judged on results and actively monitors own performance.

Target users

The centre can be used for recruitment or for management development purposes. The range of possible users include:

For management development

Headteachers of primary or secondary schools;

Senior management teams, for the purposes of whole school, team or individual development;

Officers in LEAs considering a return to senior positions in schools;

Deputy headteachers, for development purposes;

Development of those acting as appraisers in headteacher appraisal;

Open access for headteachers or deputy headteachers wishing to use the centre on a fee paying basis.

For recruitment

The LEA and/or governors can be provided with a service which may include job analysis of the current post through to production of a profile on each short-listed candidate.

The management development centre process

Before participants attend a centre they are given a list of the management criteria and competences upon which assessment at the centre is based. They are encouraged to think about their jobs *vis-à-vis* the competences as well as considering their own objectives for attendance.

Self-assessment is an integral part of the strategy. This is to ensure that decisions are not top down and imposed but involve the headteacher at all stages to ensure that they take ownership of decisions.

Participants are asked to complete self assessment schedules at three stages of the centre:

- before attending the centre;
- during the centre, incorporating feedback compiled into a self assessment file, and finally
- after completion of the centre and receipt of a written profile.

The self-assessment process is confidential to the individual who is not expected to share its contents with the centre staff. Individual participants rate themselves on a five point scale against each of the assessment criteria. Participants are informed that 'A score of 3 is 'typical' for each of the criteria as the majority of headteachers would be expected to score in this band'. Point 3 on the rating scale is defined as follows: 'Matches specification fairly well but has weaknesses in a few aspects'.

Work at the centre is usually undertaken with a group of six participants. The team of assessors arrive at a collaborative summary profile indicating each candidate's major management strengths and identifying potential development needs. A final feedback interview takes place 10-14 days after each centre. One assessor discusses the summary profile with the participant. All information is treated as confidential. The intention of the interview is to obtain a 'shared profile' which provides the basis for an individual management development plan.

It is recommended that the individual development plan is set in the context of the school development plan, and the LEAs management development strategy and programmes. The development plan should also reflect an individual's career aspirations.

The programme will shortly be acceptable for recognition for credit accumulation and transfer purposes towards award bearing programmes within the University of East London.

Assessment

Three assessors are present at each centre, providing a ratio of one assessor to two candidates. Two of the assessors are drawn from a pool of experienced headteachers. All of these assessors will have taken part in a centre themselves and will also have been trained. Other assessors come from the Education Management Group of the East London Business School, whose staff have been trained as assessors and in psychometric testing. They are registered as level II qualified test users as recognized by the British Psychological Society.

Research and quality control

The East London Business School national research project into leadership in schools is focusing initially on current tasks, human attributes and the management competences of headship. Work is being undertaken with a sample of over 200 head teachers in all school types and regions across England and Wales. The work of the project was described in a paper to the BEMAS Research Conference in March 1992 (Lyons 1992).

Reactions of participants and assessors

Head teacher participants have found the assessment centre experience a beneficial developmental exercise. An opportunity to analyse their everyday tasks and responsibilities has provided valuable insights into current job performance and possible future improvements. Assessors have also found the experience a valuable source of personal development. They have also been encouraged to improve their own managerial skills.

Conclusion

The project team emphasise that 'The Assessment and Development Centre, to be used successfully, must be seen as part of a total ongoing selection or management development process and not as an end in itself' (Lyons and Jirasinghe 1992). Regular re-evaluations are planned.

The project team has identified expense as a key problem. They are exploring various means of reducing costs without losing the essential features of the centre approach.

The centre development is part of a coherent approach to education management. In his paper to the BEMAS Research Conference (Lyons 1992) Geoffrey Lyons concludes that 'Job Analysis and Assessment and Development Centres appear to provide a way forward to building realistic theory in Education Management'.

References

Bowles, G., *Education Management Development Project Final Report* (CEMD/TEED, 1992)

Boyatzis, R. E., *The Competent Manager: a Model for Effective Performance*, (Chichester: John Wiley and Sons, 1982).

Burke, J., (Ed), *Competency Based Education and Training* (Lewes: Falmer Press, 1989).

CEMD, *Monograph on Management Development Programme including contributions to Chapter 3 – the Management Development Centre by* T. Beck, 'Development and Description'; R. O'Connor, 'Management Competences'; C. Hoy, Observer Training and an Observer's View; S. Cotton, A Participant's View, (1991).

Cleveland/ICI Head Teachers' Group, *School Management Data for Self Appraisal*, 1992.

Cleveland/ICI Head Teachers' Group, *Competences* booklet 1992

Lyons, G., 'Human Resource Development: a Focus on the Research and Theoretical Implications of Management Assessment and Assessment and Development Centres for Headteachers', Proceedings of the BEMAS Research Conference, Nottingham, March 1992 (to be published).

Lyons, G., and D. Jirasinghe, 'Headteacher Assessment and Development Centres', in *Educational Change and Development*, Summer 1992.

Chapter 6

Using the Standards in Norfolk and Kent

Background

This Chapter describes a new competence based management qualification for teachers initiated by the College of Preceptors in 1991 and trialled in Norfolk and Kent. The college is a professional association and learned society for teachers which has provided professional qualifications since it received its Royal Charter in 1849. This recent development accords with its long-standing tradition of open access and emphasis on effective performance in the workplace.

The new competences based qualification for teachers is the Associate of the College of Preceptors (Management) or ACP (Management). This is designed as a first level management qualification for teachers and others professionally concerned with education. The current participants in the programme include teachers who are exercising management responsibility for the first time as heads of department or first level pastoral post holders in secondary schools, or subject co-ordinators and deputy headteachers in primary schools. As well as attaining the ACP (Management) it is intended that participants will achieve a National Vocational Qualification (NVQ) level 4 and endorsement at certificate level (MI) by the Management Charter Initiative (MCI). There has been close co-operation with the MCI who are jointly assessing the pilot ACP (Management) programmes.

During 1992 a second level qualification is being developed in accordance with the MCI Standards at level II (MII).

The college made the deliberate decision to use the MCI Management Standards, and not to adapt them. This had the benefit of linking teachers with a nationally recognised generic management qualification.

The ACP (Management) has been developed in co-operation with local education authorities. Pilot schemes have been operating during 1991–92 in Norfolk and Kent. Further piloting will take place in 1992–93 and other pilot groups based in local education authorities or higher education institutions are being established. A number of higher education institutions have expressed interest in the ACP (Management) as an optional qualification for those of their students requiring competence-based assessment in addition to their own qualification.

Aims and objectives of the programme

The aims of the ACP (Management) programme are stated as follows:

- to enable practising teachers to obtain a recognized educational management qualification without unnecessary barriers to access;
- to provide a coherent framework within which both candidates may develop, and their employers may provide professional support;
- to make effective use of the workplace as a place of learning and professional development;
- to ensure that teachers have transferable competences as managers, fitting them to operate effectively in a variety of roles, both within, and outside education;
- to provide a structure whereby credit may be accumulated over a period, and candidates may receive credit for relevant experience gained outside teaching.

Objectives are spelt out in some detail and follow the MCI Management Standards. There has been no attempt to modify the standards. Examples of their possible application in a school context are provided. The intention, however, is that each candidate will contextualize the application of the standards for their own role and their own school.

Administration of the programme

As an awarding body, the College of Preceptors approves centres which run the ACP (Management) programmes. The principle of open access means that a course structure cannot be prescribed. It is the end result, the certification of competences, that concerns the college. Nevertheless the college does give guidance on recommended practice and provides a log book for each candidate which provides a detailed guide to the standards to be attained. Most candidates are supported by their school but in exceptional circumstances the college will make provision for unsupported candidates.

In the ACP (Management) programme the MCI framework is being used to enable a teacher to attain a national award through personal and professional development. The main source of evidence for assessment draws upon experience in the workplace. Individuals are encouraged to improve their professional contribution to the school in the process of working for a qualification. The key purpose of the programme is to help the school to achieve its objectives and continually improve its performance.

The candidate

The main onus of work is on the candidate who will be expected to collect evidence of his/her achievement of the competences. There is no specific timescale prescribed, but most candidates would wish to complete the work over a period of a full academic year.

The basis of the programme is the planning and work done by the candidate who will develop a log book or portfolio, which will become a record of learning and development over time. It will include a personal profile and evidence of competence and development including prior learning and experience.

The candidate will obtain appropriate reading and self-study materials to cover the knowledge and understanding requirements of the scheme. The college provides a list of suggested self-study materials and currently recommends the Bristol NDCEMP (National Development Centre for Educational Policy and Management) materials (NDCEMP 1991). Arrangements are being made with materials providers for materials to be cross referenced to the MCI competences and their underlying knowledge and understanding requirements. All the materials relate directly to school management.

The candidate will present the evidence in the portfolio to the headteacher who will be asked to confirm its authenticity. An assessor appointed by the approved centre will then examine the evidence and may ask to interview the candidate. During the pilot phase the verifier (or chief examiner) of the College of Preceptors will visit centres to monitor standards.

The role of the headteacher

The headteacher authenticates the evidence presented by the candidate by endorsing the record of evidence and stating whether or not in his/her view the candidate is, or is not yet competent for each element of competence. The guidelines also recommend that the headteacher should consider ways in which the work done by the candidate can best assist the school. Projects and assignments of real value to the school provide good evidence for the candidate to present for assessment, being rooted in performance in the workplace.

The mentor

A mentor, usually from the candidate's own school, is appointed, and will give advice to the candidate. The mentor may help the candidate to negotiate and plan work assignments in the school. The head has adopted the mentor role in some very small primary schools. The mentor is asked to:

- help the candidate by discussing his/her ideas for professional development throughout the programme;
- meet with the candidate at least twice a term to review progress and discuss problems; and
- assist the candidate to identify suitable work assignments and projects in the school.

The mentor's aim will be to encourage the candidate to assume individual 'ownership' of their development programme and to engage the mutual support of their workplace colleagues.

The tutor

The approved centre will provide minimal tutor support. Centres are free to devise their own support arrangements. After an initial meeting with candidates, the tutor will be available 'on call' to provide help and advice.

The assessor

Assessors are appointed by approved centres. Training has been provided by the College of Preceptors and MCI. As the scheme develops assessors will be encouraged to attain the competences for assessors outlined in the Training and Development Lead Body Standards (TDLB 1991). It is possible for a tutor to also act as an assessor, but *not* for their own candidates. The overall work of assessors is monitored by the College of Preceptors' verifier (chief examiner).

The College of Preceptors arranges regular meetings to enable tutors and assessors to exchange information and improve expertise.

The support centres

An approved centre may be a local education authority centre, a higher education institution or any other organization that meets the MCI and College of Preceptors requirements.

The pilot centres have provided the venue for briefing of head-teachers and mentors and for meetings of candidates. Each centre has considerable freedom to devise its own support structure.

The log book

The Occupational Standards for Managers have been described in Chapter Three. The college provides guidance on their application in education. A detailed log book provides the candidate with guidance on sources and forms of evidence for the elements of competence within each of the nine units of competence.

The log book is being revised in the light of experience in the pilot groups, and it is intended that a build up of examples of work done may produce a data base of examples of good evidence under each of the elements of competence.

The pilot programmes in Norfolk and Kent are described below. The Norfolk programme began later than the Kent pilot and the early developments are described. The Kent contribution is a thorough analysis of the initial pilot by Phil Holden who managed the Kent ACP (Management) programme. Of 19 teachers initially enrolled for the Kent programme, seven have completed it successfully and two more are well on the way to completing their portfolio of evidence. The account of issues arising in the first pilot programme provides useful guidance for the next phase of the pilot scheme in Kent and elsewhere.

The Norfolk ACP (Management) programme

Norfolk advertised the ACP (Management) course to teachers in primary schools in the Autumn of 1991. The target participants were holders of co-ordinator posts and deputy heads in the primary phase. They were informed that the course would be competence-led and would involve the assessment of prior learning. Candidates would have to demonstrate that they are competent in accordance with the MCI Standards. They were also informed that assessment would involve:

- reports based on a case study and a problem set for consideration;
- a review of a log book kept by a candidate; and
- the assessment of work based activities authenticated by the employer.

Candidates would prepare for the qualification at work, with provision for open learning. They would not be required to be away from school to attend the course. The County INSET (In-service education and training) Centre was the base from which the Board of Study, drawn both from the LEA and the College of Preceptors, would administer, run and accredit the course.

Implementation

In January 1992 a first cohort of eight candidates began their course. They were all from a range of small, medium and large first, primary and middle schools. They represented a good geographical spread across the county.

External support

LEA inspectors and advisers acted as tutors. Each tutor provided support for two candidates. They organized for participants two general meetings in Norwich. Headteachers were also invited to one meeting. Tutors visited each school once per term. Candidates had a list of names, addresses and telephone numbers to facilitate networking. They were also able to telephone the tutor for advice.

The self-study materials provided by the LEA were from the University of Bristol (NDCEMP 1991).

Assessment of evidence presented by candidates was undertaken by tutors acting as assessors. They did not assess the work of the two people for whom they provided tutor support.

In-school support

The headteacher has the task of certifying that the evidence presented by the candidate is valid. In addition heads are encouraged to consider ways in which the work done by the candidate might assist the school. The candidates agreed that the headteacher should act as mentor in every case.

The log book

Each Norfolk school has an Apple Macintosh computer for administrative purposes. At an early stage one candidate suggested that the log book should be on disk. This was agreed readily. Candidates have completed their assignments on disk and in doing so have also demonstrated competence in the use of the school's information system, having learnt the necessary information technology skills.

Comments from the schools

The reactions of candidates have been positive. They have found the experience of using their normal work as a vehicle for providing evidence of competence a spur to professional development. Some headteachers have been able to use the work done by the candidate to further the development of the school. In one case the headteacher has used a report by the candidate to the governors to introduce a regular and more effective liaison between the governors and the school staff. In that case the governors have also acquired a greater interest in staff development.

Comments from the project team

The team have identified the following advantages of the scheme.

- It is much more cost effective than a traditionally taught course. There is no need for supply cover. Travel and subsistence costs are also minimized.
- It has benefits for the institution as well as the individual. Tasks are negotiated in the school and can be linked to the School Development Plan.
- Tasks are related to daily practice and are practical and relevant.
- The scheme does not involve any dislocation in an individual's timetable, the school programme or the teaching of pupils.

- The course provides nationally recognized accreditation.

The Norfolk team are planning improvements to this pilot scheme. It will be necessary to provide simulations and other opportunities for school managers who are not able to demonstrate evidence from the workplace for certain competences. The other requirement is to tackle the need for additional support to people who need further knowledge and understanding of management. This issue is being pursued by Norfolk and by the College of Preceptors with some providers of self-study materials.

Accreditation issues

Norfolk, like other LEAs, is developing accredited courses as a major part of their INSET provision. The number of accredited courses being developed and offered by LEAs and higher education institutions is likely to be subject to critical review in terms of academic rigour and external assessment.

The Norfolk strategy is to develop the team of assessors so that they can serve several competence based in-service programmes including the management programmes in education. In this way a competent team of assessors, trained to meet the Training and Development Lead Body competence requirements can help to guarantee a sufficient rigour in the competence based programmes.

Norfolk is considering a board which will review and plan the variety of courses and assist the exchange of best practice by means of:

- liaison between the various providers of accredited courses to avoid overlap and duplication;
- rationalization of use of resources, including venues;
- co-ordination of information flow to schools.

Associated developments and future plans

It is proposed to enlarge the cohort next year and also to extend the scheme through to the secondary phase. This scheme must been seen alongside other developments in Norfolk. A core of four assessors on this course has been extended to six. Other related courses are now using these experienced assessors on other developments. These include:

An accredited course 'Reading in the Primary School'. This provides an ACP which allows teachers to update their skills in reading. This is partly a taught course but it is based upon units of competence, appropriate performance requirements and sources of evidence and the requirement to prepare a reflective journal or log. The units of competence have been devised in Norfolk to cover the specific competences required.

The Post 16 Curriculum Management Programme. This provides mentor training which involves the maintenance of a development portfolio, assessment and accreditation processes and other features of a competence based scheme.

The Sheffield Polytechnic FE Management Development Course. This programme was organized to meet the needs of FE institutions, and the LEA youth and adult education services. The programme is built on learning contracts, the support of mentors and the build up of a management development file by each candidate who accumulates points towards either a certificate or diploma in education management.

The Norfolk strategy is to develop the team of assessors so that they can serve several competence based in-service programmes including the management programmes in education.

Norfolk also use the Open University professional development in education course, RSA and other qualifications. They also use the Oxford EAC assessment centres for aspects of deputy head professional development. The county personnel department is also involved in competence based programmes, some of them in education.

The Kent ACP (Management) programme

The Kent co-ordinator, Phil Holden, writes as follows: 'Tom Peters said during a visit to Kent "perception is all there is" and Kent's experience exemplifies this'.

Do teachers see themselves as 'managers'?

Teachers (and sometimes headteachers) are quite happy to see themselves as classroom, curriculum or budget managers. Many of them seem to have difficulty with the notion of being referred to as a 'school manager'.

If a management development programme is based upon the MCI standards which describe what 'managers' do this immediately presents a problem. This reluctance to call oneself a manager is not reflected in other public and private organizations where being a manager has status. The success of the ACP (Management) scheme is dependent upon acceptance of the MCI standards and the individual's perception of management and being a manager. Some people who found this a perpetual problem eventually withdrew from the programme, or did not submit their portfolio at the first opportunity to do so.

What do teachers expect from a course?

The Kent programme was advertised as a course leading to a qualification – the ACP (Management). This definition proved to be unhelpful. People expected to be taught by tutors to a predetermined syllabus. They also expected accreditation to come at the end in the form of an assessed, specially commissioned document.

In our 'course' these normalities were not present. 'We are not here to teach you...but we expect you to learn from experience', said the tutor. 'We shall help you to assess your individual needs and supporting your development within your current job role...through the compilation of a portfolio of your past and current experience we shall accredit your competences, knowledge and understanding'. All good School Management Task Force stuff, we thought! The participants sat slightly bemused by this. Bemusement turned to bewilderment when we gave them a list of units and elements of competence with, in our view, an inadequate explanation of them. We did provide, on loan, some Bristol University materials (Bristol).

It was the 'MCI speak' that foxed them. The largely impenetrable statements in the standards should not have been pushed at an unsuspecting audience without considerable preparation. It is essential to alter perceptions of the programme before asking people to tackle the standards. Two shifts in perception is too much.

There is also a perplexing dichotomy. On the one hand we wholeheartedly subscribe to the Task Force view that people develop close to the job and that develpopment is essentially about specific individual needs. These needs are closely related to the specific role of the individual within a specific job context. On the other hand, the whole thrust and philosophy of the MCI Standards is that they are generic and apply to each and every management context. The accreditation of competences is a process of applying these predetermined standards to one's own specific context. The development needs of an individual are therefore analysed in terms of the standards rather than the individual and his or her role. The combination of this juxtaposition requires the programme leader to acquire a solid perception of how this will work and how to present this to the participants.

In our case, this problem became easier as time went by. It was no longer a problem for those who completed the programme. It was another factor that lost some people along the way however. For the next group we propose to focus more upon the competence related needs analysis at the beginning of the programme *after* we have spent time discussing the conceptual framework of the course.

The role of mentors and headteachers

This was the first ACP pilot scheme. It had been hoped to train mentors via the College of Preceptors but funds were not available. This proved to be a significant weakness in the Kent programme as the position of mentors and their support role was never firmly established. There was lack of internal support for some candidates and some confusion in other cases about what the mentor should do.

The role of the headteacher in the programme was also confused. As ultimate line manager the headteacher is expected to authenticate evidence submitted by the candidate following discussion, but most did not get adequate briefing and found it difficult to witness the authenticity of the material. Headteachers and mentors should be involved at a very early stage and as soon as the needs analysis has been undertaken by candidates.

Compiling portfolios

The portfolio is not a familiar medium for teachers, who are more used to examinations. The portfolio's diary-like characteristics, the need to keep notes of activities and self-reflection, was far removed from the previous experience of most candidates. Tutors had to spend a great deal of time going over evidence with candidates to help them to see their activities in relation to the standards. We also ran several group sessions in which we went through the elements and units systematically. Ample opportunity needs to be created for this type of individual and group support.

Assessment perceptions

Having all been teachers, we understsand what assessment is and how to go about it. We know all about marks, grades, percentages and rankings for a written piece of work. Assessing portfolio evidence couldn't be more different. The assessment of competence against the standards is that you are either 'competent' or 'not yet competent'. There is no partial success, except that you can pick off units of competence and get them credited as you go along. Competence is certainly not related to the volume of evidence presented.

The perplexing simplicity of this either/or assessment places a greater emphasis upon the candidate to find enough evidence to demonstrate competence. There is no definitive answer to the question 'what is enough?' This places the assessor under pressure to be clear about what he or she is looking for. The MCI Standards help because they have clearly identified range statements and performance criteria. It is still no easy matter for you to say as an assessor that an individual is competent in a given skill, will be competent in the future and in any other working context and that they have the knowledge and understanding to transfer their competence.

Assessors need to be adequately trained in the role and assessment techniques, to be conversant with the standards and to have some first hand experience of the process in order to be confident assessors. They need support in the role before going solo. Such support was provided in the pilot scheme.

Both assessors and candidates need to feel confident about the process. More time will be spent at the beginning of the next programme explaining the process and 'training' the candidates in self assessment techniques.

Conclusion

Testing the ACP (Management) programme in Kent has revealed five major issues around the perceptions of educators about the MCI and NCVQ processes. The piloting of the ACP has been a rewarding learning experience for me, my colleagues and the participants and the lessons learnt are already being integrated into the next programme. The experience has triggered five wider questions:

1. To what extent are teachers and headteachers 'managers' in the nationally accepted sense?

2. How can we break away from our need for courses which involve off-site tuition and move towards the recommendations of the School Management Task Force for school based development?
3. As a result of the above, how are the roles and responsibilities of headteachers and mentors changing in schools as they accept more responsibility for supporting and appraising their staff?
4. Will the use of portfolios of achievement widen as appraisal and school-based development becomes embedded in an increasingly non-LEA supported environment?
5. How will schools and management trainers find the time and money to successfully support competence based assessment processes for school teachers and managers?

Reflections on the first two pilot schemes

The unfamiliar MCI language presents a potential barrier for teachers, who need considerable help to apply the standards to their own context. Examples of how the MCI performance criteria apply in school situations has helped people to apply the scheme to their own job.

There is a need for good quality self-study materials. This will become particularly important at middle management level (MII) where a greater depth of underlying knowledge is required. Good materials are available already and new materials are being produced, some of which will have regard to the needs of competence-based approaches.

The initial pilot schemes have demonstrated the varied ways in which individuals, schools and local education authorities can use the ACP (Management) programme. Teachers are attracted to professional development which draws largely upon experience in the workplace, once the language and perceptions of the standards are understood.

The college is convinced of the value of management standards at levels I and II. It has yet to be convinced that MCI Standards for senior managers are feasible. An alternative route to an academic MBA is being explored.

Another major problem has been identified – that of funding. The devolution of budgets to individual schools makes it increasingly difficult to pay for support of activities that seem to benefit one teacher on the staff.

References

College of Preceptors, *ACP Management pilot Log Book*, (1991).

Hall, V., M. Wallace, and T. Hill, *Management Self-Development*, (Bristol: NDCEMP, University of Bristol, 1991).

Training and Development Lead Body, *National Standards for Training and Development. Supplement: Standards for Assessment and Verification*, August 1991.

Chapter 7

Using the Occupational Standards for Managers – Calderdale and Manchester Polytechnic

This Chapter provides examples of the use of the MCI Standards in two different contexts. In each case the standards have been used in their generic form and have not been contextualized for use in schools.

Piloting the management standards in Calderdale LEA

This account draws considerably upon the work of John Jagger, General Inspector for Management Development in Calderdale. The Calderdale experience is described fully in an Open University Reader (Jagger 1991).

Background

Three coincidences are said to have triggered the developments in Calderdale. These were the appointment of a General Inspector for Management Development, the recognition by headteachers of the implication of local management of schools and the relocation of a firm of management consultants (Qudos UK) who were piloting the Occupational Standards for Managers.

The local education authority was looking for relevant, cost effective, on the job training to be of immediate benefit to individuals and institutions and also of help to people for their future roles. Qudos were looking for partners to pilot the standards.

Initial phase of development

A pilot group of 24 volunteers included staff from two 11-18 comprehensive schools (department heads, co-ordinators and deputy heads), some primary school heads and deputies, and four LEA officers. These volunteers joined managers from other occupations on a development programme. Qudos provided an introductory workshop on the standards and a further workshop on their application to individual's work practices. Action learning sets of eight were established. People from outside education were appointed as advisers/mentors to these action learning sets. Participants then completed a comprehensive portfolio of evidence of competence cross-referenced to the standards.

Very early in the project the importance of personal competences was recognized. These were not assessed formally for accreditation but proved to be useful for a variety of developmental purposes. Personal competences enabled the standards to be used in the following ways:

- to provide a means of matching an individual job to a comprehensive analysis of what might be expected of a manager and then to provide a training analysis for possible action;
- to provide within action learning sets a basis for discussion about alternative strategies of evidence-generation or personal development;
- to encourage groups or individuals to consider the motives behind described behaviours;
- to provide as objective benchmarks as possible against which to measure one's current performance and seek to improve it;
- to construct systems to ensure appropriate responses to recurring issues; and
- to provide a common reference for the individual and their assessor.

Additional uses of the standards have included production of job descriptions, providing a 'contract' to describe the focus of appraisal and writing descriptions or contracts for desired training outcomes.

Action learning sets

These had the purpose of exploiting the mutual support that individuals gain from networking. They have proved useful for clarification of issues, motivation and as occasions when strategies could be discussed and concerns shared.

The mentor/adviser

These were experienced managers from occupational sectors other than education. Their three main tasks were:

- to ensure that the group was properly managed and supported;
- to ask those 'naive questions' which outsiders can raise, which enable participants to reflect on their own practice;
- to motivate and promote a desire to improve performance and establish high management expectations by the group.

Mentor/adviser support was considered to be crucial when individuals had to describe what they do and why in relation to the standards. Group members also needed considerable help to provide evidence of competence.

Aspects of assessment

The assessors had the task of determining how far previous learning or experience had been internalized and was being reflected in an individual manager's behaviour.

Working for assessment kept many candidates on task even though the prime purpose was developmental. There was concern initially that a non-education assessor might not understand the context in which participants operated. Most candidates for assessment saw the need to explain the context as a challenge rather than a threat.

The second phase of development

The diploma level of Standards (MII) was introduced. These assess a more senior level of management than MI.

During the second phase further training was provided for first phase participants who would act in future as mentors/advisers.

The second phase programme also introduced the following features:

- a management project on a priority topic identified within the development plan of the school or department;
- the addition of a personal competences model and the keeping of critical incident diaries by participants.

Third phase development

The project will be extended as an entitlement to all primary school deputies. The project team feel this group to be at risk as local management of schools widens the skills gap between head and deputy. It is important in their view to encourage geniune shared leadership and management.

Observations of the project team

Candidates found the generic language of the standards difficult. However, the experience of discussing the standards and the job context with mentor/advisers from outside education provided a useful challenge and stimulus to development. Participants also gained in confidence as they realized that their management role was equal to that of others. One person described their reactions as follows: 'for the first time feeling respectable among other managers from different contexts'.

Jagger states that there are difficulties for educators because the MCI Standards put greater restrictions on them than managers in very different contexts. The management of learning and the learning environment is not easily accommodated. One example is the management of students which is not recognized as management within the standards. The hierarchical nature of the MCI model is very different from the management style and practices of schools.

The standards are focused on accreditation rather than development. They also demand an enormous workload for all concerned. Nevertheless Calderdale sees considerable benefit in the use of the standards for development purposes.

The Calderdale comments on the possible applications of the standards in schools are considered further in Chapter Eleven.

Manchester Polytechnic: the use of MCI Standards in competence-based education management development

MCI developments in three local education authorities

The Education Management Centre at the Polytechnic is using the MCI Management Standards framework to provide management development for teachers from three local education authorities in the north west of England: Bolton, Tameside and Rochdale. The aim has been to try to achieve the guidelines outlined in the School Management Task Force report (SMTF 1990). That report stated, 'The school, especially the head and governors, has the responsibility for developing its capacity to manage itself, and to develop its managers'.

The Manchester team were attracted to the MCI approach because of the following features:

- a framework of managerial competences;
- the development of people in the workplace;
- the opportunity to empower individuals to assess and meet their own developmental needs;
- the acknowledgement that performance on the job is more important than knowledge acquisition alone; and
- the opportunity to recognize individual enhanced performance through accreditation.

The pilot project offers accreditation at level 1 (M1) using the MCIs 'Crediting Competence' workbook (MCI 1991). Initially the project recruited over one hundred teachers from the primary, secondary and further education sectors. Participants work at establishing their competence as managers, using the standards as a framework for examining their practice and for seeking ways of developing themselves in areas where they are deemed 'not yet competent'.

Evidence that participants have met the performance criteria is collected and presented in a portfolio which is then assessed with the aid of an assessment interview. Workshops, or action learning sets, support the programme and the production of the portfolio. Each workshop group has an adviser.

Evaluation of the project

This section describes the work done as part of a survey to evaluate the experience of teachers who had used the MCI Standards I. This account draws extensively upon the project report (Bowles 1992).

Aims of the survey

The survey investigated:

- the applicability of the standards to the work of teachers;
- the degree to which the standards assist the identification of training and development needs; and
- ways in which participants can be helped to develop knowledge and understanding to match future as well as present demands.

In addition, the survey examined the claims of MCI Standards to promote flexible and cost effective management development.

The survey process

The MCI scheme in Bolton began in September 1991 and it was possible to survey that cohort by questionnaire as they started the programme and to review their early impressions against a further questionnaire distributed in March 1992.

In Tameside and Rochdale the programme had begun in 1990 and participants were at various stages towards or at completion of the programme. Some Tameside participants had also taken part in the earlier CEMD profiling project (described in Chapter Five) and were able to use evidence from their management development profile from that project in their submissions to MCI. A cross section of participants together with a number of heads were interviewed to gain an employer's view. In addition local authority advisers with management responsibility were interviewed. The regional perspective was further examined by discussion with those responsible for management development in Cheshire, Knowsley, Oldham, Salford, Stockport and Wirral LEAs where profile-based provision was being considered.

Outside the region, Calderdale LEA was also consulted. The outcome of discussions at two national profiling conferences at the University of Nottingham were also considered.

Outcomes of the survey

All participants were volunteers and there were differences of approach in the three LEAs. It was possible however to come to some clear conclusions. The survey revealed that:

- the MCI Standards provide a comprehensive, valuable and useable framework for organizing and accrediting past experience;
- this audit of managerial contributions is personally satisfying and potentially useful in gaining recognition for work undertaken within organizations;
- local education authorities are beginning to adopt the approach as the central focus of their management development programme; and
- the process of collecting and presenting evidence of competence is time-consuming. However, an APL (accreditation of prior learning) approach to a qualification probably takes up less time than traditional management development programmes;
- there is a danger that the aggregation of evidence can become an end in itself but where it leads to the creation of learning opportunities it is considered highly beneficial;
- support for those compiling their portfolio of evidence is crucial;
- it is important that senior management create and facilitate development opportunities;
- the MCI specifications have high face validity with participants and appear relevant and comprehensive in an educational context;
- participants feel empowered by the process and more confident in asking for additional experience where there appear to be competence gaps;
- the approach offers a basis for structured linking of individual development and organizational development; the approach offers good data to inform appraisal and other personnel management processes and allows better planning of staff development and deployment;
- with more emphasis on inspection and a need for clearer criteria and benchmarks for performance the MCI Standards provide a helpful framework;
- the portfolio approach has much to offer as a means of giving coherence to current career development and progression.

The evaluation report does have some reservations about the MCI approach, concluding that the approach appears to favour the organized and documented managerial approach over the intuitive and may work in favour of those with well-ordered filing cabinets. For some the language of the standards can be initially off-putting but for those who persevere with the contextualization and grapple with the language the very process can be highly developmental.

Comments on specific aspects of the MCI approach

Assessment

The assessment of portfolios has presented issues of the criteria to be applied and the need for assessor training. The quality of the programme depends upon a consistent application of criteria and assessors need opportunities to meet together to compare experiences.

Management self-development

The process could favour the meticulous administrator over the 'manager by walking about'. A work place mentor might redress this balance, but there was not, as yet, sufficient widespread understanding of the MCI process for this to occur.

The nature of the MCI documentation puts considerable weight on the collection of evidence. Any attempt to assess the added learning that has taken place must depend on a degree of subjective judgement on the part of the assessor. This might compromise the intended objectivity of the functional analysis approach.

Funding and timing

This proved to be an expensive process when the overall costs of advising, portfolio preparation and assessment are taken into account. There is a problem of reconciling the self-paced nature of the profile with the calendar fixed nature of course entry dates and annual budget allocations.

Accreditation

The possibility of giving candidates exemption from year one of the Polytechnic MSc Education Management course is being considered.

Support for the process

The process requires support and resourcing on at least three levels to be cost effective:

- at a one to one group mentoring level;
- at a group (action learning set) level; and
- at an organization level where senior management creates a climate of support and encourages staff development.

Manchester Polytechnic is continuing 'to explore the portfolio, competences, mentoring and action learning methodologies which, when combined, might offer a more sustainable, school-based management development process'. (Beck 1992).

Participant intentions

Those who managed the introduction of the process saw signs that participants tended to divide into 'those who saw the main purpose of the standards as retrospective, enabling past and present work to be accredited' and 'those who saw the exercise as encouraging critical reflection with the intention of refining or redefining future practice and direction'.

The language of the standards

The language of the standards provided an obstacle for those on the initial trials. However, some teachers welcomed comparability with those outside education and found the contextualization of the language challenging. Others saw the language as an uneccessary complication 'importing values and attitudes that are uncomfortable to education'.

Support for individuals

The developmental aim was 'considerably facilitated where there was the opportunity to discuss the profile with others, whether peers, people from other schools, advisers, senior managers or tutors from outside the authority'. Obtaining such support was a greater problem for primary school teachers than for those from secondary schools.

Respondents liked the approach to learning offered. The survey concluded that 'The provision of what could be seen as a set of short term targets for development could be a very practical strategy for development when the participants are under such competing pressure for their time as is the case with most teachers presently'.

The survey team believe that it is important for reflection to take place. Otherwise the exercise could degenerate into a checklist and paper collecting exercise.

The standards and training needs

Respondents were able to confirm that the standards did help them to 'relate training and development needs to employment requirements'. The standards helped them to

- evaluate their own jobs;
- identify strengths and weaknesses;
- highlight gaps in their experience;
- recognize the part that others played in achieving school objectives;
- clarify roles and relationships; and
- realize the benefit of regular review and audit.

Teachers saw the possibility of the profile assisting teacher control of the appraisal process.

There was little evidence, as yet, that the training needs identified were being used by schools or authorities formally to help decisions about allocation of INSET opportunities or funds.

Accreditation was seen to be important in that it gave the process status and helped to motivate staff.

Organizational development

There were several cases where the process had led to developments in the school and use of the standards by groups or by the whole staff. The survey concluded that 'Such co-operative arrangements were more likely to take place where there was already a developed process of planning and review and a clear allocation of roles and responsibilities, and where the culture of the school encouraged open debate and regular consultation, and where senior teachers took an active interest in the development of the staff'.

General conclusions

The survey concluded that 'The MCI Standards offer an extensive and detailed set of benchmarks for management development which can be usefully employed in an educational context to organize and accredit past experience and for the development and extension of new competences'. However, considerable support is required at one to one level in school, at group level within or across schools and at an organizational level with the active involvement of senior staff. Participants also require careful briefing. Benefits are seen for individuals, schools and LEAs in terms of improving the quality of school management.

References

Beck, T., 'Finding Out How You Measure Up', in *The Times Educational Supplement* 27 March 1992.

Bowles, G., *Evaluation of the Use of MCI Standards in Competence-Based Education Management Development*, (TEED/CEMD, 1992).

Department of Education and Science, School Management Task Force, *Developing School Management: The Way Forward*, (London: HMSO, 1990).

Jagger, J., *MCI and Educational Management; The Calderdale/Qudos Project*, (Open University Reader, 1991).

Jagger, J., 'Enhancing the Skills of Managers: Calderdale LEA and the Management Charter Initiative', in *Managing Schools Today*, Autumn 1991.

MCI, *Crediting Competence*, 1991.

Chapter 8

Developing and Using the Standards — School Management South

Peter Earley, Director, School Management Competences
Project.

Background

This project was initiated by School Management South (SMS), a
regional consortium of 14 local education authorities in southeast
England (Berkshire, Bexley, Bromley, Croydon, East Sussex,
Hampshire, Isle of Wight, Kent, Kingston, Merton, Richmond,
Surrey, Sutton and West Sussex). The consortium was set up in 1988 to
develop a more strategic approach to school management development for senior staff in the region's 3,600 schools.

The School Management Competences Project was one of eight
pilot programmes designed to promote management development in
schools. The project was sponsored by the Department of Employment (DE) through its occupational standards programme managed
by the Training, Enterprise and Education Directorate (formerly the
Training Agency). With funds from the DE and SMS, the two year
pilot project analysed the functions of school management in order to
derive standards which define explicitly what is expected of effective
management performance.

Aims and management of the project

The prime aim of the project was 'to analyse school management functions in order to ascertain school-based (employment-led) standards for effective school management in both primary and secondary phases of education and for all professionals with a major responsibility for the work of other adults in the school'.

The project was also to develop and implement, on a trial basis, associated systems of assessment, management development and accreditation. This work was to be piloted in a small number of schools and local education authorities in the region.

The project team consisted of a full-time project director, two seconded headteachers, and, for part of the time, a senior research fellow. The team received regular support from the directors of SMS and a project steering committee. The committee met every three months and its members were chosen to resemble an industry-lead body for the education sector, including employer and professional association representatives. The project team began their work in April 1990 and produced the final report two years later (Earley 1992).

The competences model

The School Management Competences Project followed a framework and methodology developed by the Department of Employment National Standards programme.

The School Management Standards, like the MCI generic standards described in Chapter Three are expressed as outcomes and provide benchmarks or specifications against which school management performance can be assessed. They have the same components as any set of competence statements or standards that are being used to form the basis of national vocational qualifications (NVQs) standards: key purpose; key functions or roles; units of competence; elements of competence; performance criteria and range statements.

The SMS standards are shown in Figures 8.1(a) and 8.1(b).

Figure 8.1(a) *The school management standards*

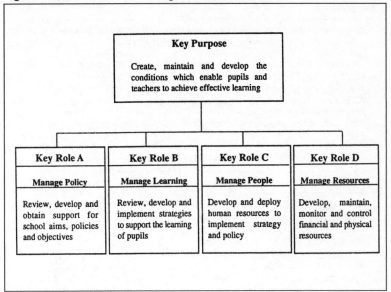

Developing the standards

The SMS project team adopted the approach of other Department of Employment projects and made use of functional analysis workshops. In these workshops, current practitioners come together, and with the help of a facilitator or consultant, define the key purpose of school management. The functions required to achieve the key purpose were then defined and units and elements of competence identified. The resulting standards should define specifically what is expected in school management performance.

The SMS project drew on the methodology developing in other Department of Employment occupational standards projects and was able to secure the services of consultants who had helped develop the Management Charter Initiative (MCI) Standards.

Functional analysis workshops

Five two-day functional analysis workshops took place; two with the primary sector and three with the secondary sector. The primary phase

Figure 8.1(b) *The school management standards: units and elements of competence*

A1 Review, develop and present school aims, policies and objectives
● A1.1 Identify opportunities and constraints on aims, policies and objectives; ● A1.2 Encourage discussion of school aims, policies and objectives; ● A1.3 Develop school aims, policies and objectives; ● A1.4 Seek agreement and disseminate school aims, policies and objectives; ● A1.5 Evaluate and review effectiveness of school aims, policies and objectives

A2 Develop supportive relationships with pupils, staff, parents, governors and the community
● A2.1 Identify problems and opportunities; ● A2.2 Develop and maintain positive relationships with interested parties; ● A2.3 Promote the school and its services; ● A2.4 Recruit pupils and operate admissions policy; ● A2.5 Evaluate and review relationships and promotion of school

B1 Review, develop and implement means for supporting pupils' learning
● B1.1 Identify learning needs of individuals and groups of pupils; ● B1.2 Review, develop and agree means of planning and supporting learning; ● B1.3 Implement learning programmes

B2 Monitor and evaluate learning programmes
● B2.1 Monitor delivery of learning programmes; ● B2.2 Evaluate effectiveness of learning programmes

C1 Recruit and select teaching and non-teaching staff
● C1.1 Define future personnel requirements; ● C1.2 Determine recruitment methods; ● C1.3 Determine specifications to secure quality people; ● C1.4 Assess and select candidates against team and school requirements

C2 Develop teams, individuals and self to enhance performance
● C2.1 Develop and improve teams through planning and activities; ● C2.2 Identify, review and improve development activities for individuals; ● C2.3 Develop oneself within the job role; ● C2.4 Evaluate and improve the development processes used

C3 Plan, allocate and evaluate work carried out by teams, individuals and self
● C3.1 Set and update work objectives for teams and individuals; ● C3.2 Plan activities and determine work methods to achieve objectives; ● C3.3 Negotiate work allocation and evaluate teams, individuals and self against objectives; ● C3.4 Provide feedback to teams and individuals on their performance

C4 Create, maintain and enhance effective working relationships
● C4.1 Establish and maintain the trust and support of one's staff; ● C4.2 Establish and maintain the trust and support of one's immediate manager; ● C4.3 Establish and maintain relationships with colleagues; ● C4.4 Identify and minimize interpersonal conflict; ● C4.5 Implement disciplinary and grievance procedures; ● C4.6 Counsel staff

D1 Secure effective resource allocation
● D1.1 Identify resources necessary to support learning; ● D1.2 Develop and maintain means of generating income and resources; ● D1.3 Justify proposals for expenditure; ● D1.4 Negotiate and agree budgets; ● D1.5 Establish and maintain supply of resources

D2 Monitor and control the use of resources
● D2.1 Control costs and enhance value; ● D2.2 Monitor and control activities against budgets; ● D2.3 Create and maintain the necessary environment for effective learning

---

led the secondary by some three months. Nearly 50 participants from a variety of management positioned within schools attended the workshops during school time. The project team prepared preliminary background papers for the workshops and were actively involved in them.

At the first workshop, the definition of the key purpose of primary school management was achieved, but time limitations restricted the work on the documentation of key functions, and this was pursued in the second workshop. The secondary sector workshops benefited from the earlier work and it quickly became apparent that there were few differences between the sectors in terms of the functions of school management.

Following the workshops further information was gained from participants by correspondence, especially in relation to performance criteria. The project consultant, assisted by the project team, was able to produce a set of draft standards. These were modified and put out to a wider audience for consultation in the spring of 1991.

The project team also undertook a number of mini case studies in eight primary schools and four secondary schools. A number of staff were interviewed in each school at all levels (including probationary teachers) in the primary schools, but mainly senior managers in the secondary schools. The workshop key purpose statement was used as the starting point for most primary school discussions. Teachers were asked what constituted core management competences. These initial case study interviews were open ended and wide ranging. In later visits to secondary schools discussion focused more specifically on the evolving SMS standards and performance criteria.

The case study interview data were used to help develop the standards and give prominence to certain funtions, eg 'managing people' and 'developing teams'. It was clear that the school visits helped to ground the analysis in the reality of school management and pointed to what practitioners themselves regarded as key competences.

The development of the SMS standards aimed to maximize congruence with the MCI Management Standards 'where the evidence allowed it'. The project team drew upon the experience of the Calderdale LEA where educationists were participating in an MCI/APL (accreditation of prior learning) 'experienced' managers pilot certificate programme (Jagger 1991). Further work was done to examine the relevance and applicability of the MCI Management Standards to schools. The consultants working with Calderdale were asked by SMS to contextualize for schools the MCI range indicators for Management 1 (first line managers) and Management 2 (middle managers). In addition, some headteachers in the SMS case studies were asked to comment upon the MCI standards. Headteacher members of the project team also undertook a critical analysis of the generic management standards. Finally, a two day workshop with heads and deputies provided further useful information on the Management 2 standards and their applicability to education.

Overview of the School Management Standards

The relationship between the School Management Standards and the MCI Management Standards is a close one. The SMS standards consist of four key functions or roles, 10 units and 41 elements, 23 of which have been adapted from the MCI standards and contextualized for the schools sector. A comparison of the two sets of standards shows that the SMS model has used the key function 'Manage people'. Some of the units and elements from MCI(M2) have been incorporated with the addition of an element 'Determine recruitment methods'. Some of the MCI units and elements from the key functions 'Manage finance' and 'Manage operations' have been amalgamated by SMS and are referred to as 'Manage resources'. The MCI key function 'Manage information' has not been directly used although aspects of information management, problem solving and leading meetings are to be found throughout the SMS key function 'Manage policy'.

It must be emphasized that the SMS project was attempting to draw a map of the *totality* of school management functions including senior management functions. At that time MCI had no senior management (M3) model developed. This explained some of the divergence between the SMS and MCI standards and why the former attempted to give some consideration to strategic management, development planning and policy formulation – usually associated with the functions of senior management.

The project and its outcomes

The School Management Standards, which were refined and developed after receiving feedback from over 90 schools, were not the only 'product' of the project. There was also a 'Guide to Evidence Collection and Assessment' which was produced for schools. It helps them to collect evidence against the School Management Standards. The first part of the guide provides information about the principles and practices underpinning the assessment process associated with competence-based qualifications. It also offers advice on the compilation of a portfolio of evidence. Part two of the guide provides more specific assessment guidance in relation to the units and elements of competence. The guide recognizes that the standards can be used for a variety of purposes: self-assessment, appraisal, team or school review, or, when linked to award bearing courses, accreditation.

The final report to the Department of Employment provides an account of the project's development and outcomes. A major part of the report is concerned with accreditation and assessment issues. Summaries of reports from higher education providers suggest how the standards might be linked to existing or new qualifications in school management.

The final report also documents the experiences of seven pilot schools, and 25 managers in them, who field tested or trialled the evolving standards. The report finally considers the national applicability of the project's outcomes (Earley 1992).

Assessment and accreditation

The assessment of school management competences formed an important part of the project and was considered by an assessment working party. This group, drawn from local education authorities, higher education (HE), a distance learning company and the Department of Employment, was partly responsible for drawing up assessment guidelines and range statements. In doing so they took account of the MCI guidelines on assessment (MCI 1990).

It was not the purpose of the project that the School Management Standards should be used for certification purposes. It was intended, however, that the project would inform any assessment system for accreditation. Accreditation research was an important part of the project's work. Indeed two HE members of the working party were asked to give an indication of how the evidence of competence collected by the pilot school participants might be accredited within any new or existing school management qualifications. The findings of these higher education institutions are recorded in the final report of the project. It is interesting to note that since the publication of the SMS standards at least one institute of higher education has decided to accredit them.

The assessment working party provided guidance on assessment and the collection of evidence to SMS pilot schools. This complemented the training given to participants which had included an introduction to the assessment principles and practices underpinning competence-based qualifications. Participants were made aware of the crucial roles of mentors and assessors. At a later stage all assessors were given relevant extracts of the revised Training and Development Lead Body Standards.

Arrangements in schools for mentoring and assessing

Arrangements for mentoring and assessing are shown in the following diagrams:

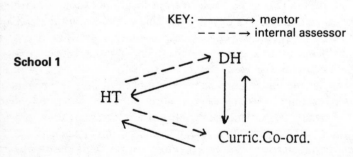

NB *Where possible arrangements for internal assessment will be made within the school, whilst the external assessor function will be undertaken by the project team.*

KEY: ———→ mentor
- - - - → internal assessor

School 1   DH

HT

Curric.Co-ord.

The head will be 'internally' assessed by another (neighbouring) pilot school head.

School 2

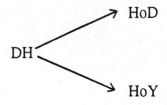

HT ——————→ DH

The arrangements for the internal assessment of the head will be the same as for School 1.

School 3

HT ——————→ DH

The arrangements for internal assessment have not, as yet, been finalized.

School 4

DH ⟨ →HoD
     →HoY

It is hoped that the head of a neighbouring pilot school will act as internal assessor.

School 5

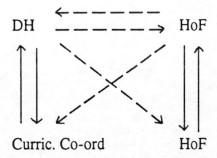

DH ⟷ HoF

Curric. Co-ord   HoF

The four individuals in this school have split into two pairs for mentoring purposes. The deputy head and head of year 6 are acting as internal assessors.

School 6

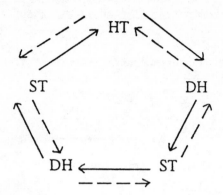

The arrangements within School 6 are that each of the five members of the senior management team are acting as mentors and internal assessors to two individuals. However, the mentoring and assessing is being carried out on a reciprocal basis (e.g. the head is assessing the senior teacher who in turn is acting as mentor to the head. Meanwhile, the head is mentoring one of the deputies).

School 7

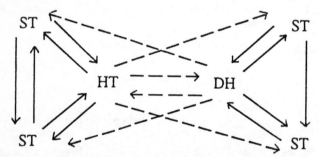

Within this school the members of the SMT have joined one of two groups of three, with one member of each (the head and the deputy) acting as internal assessor for the other group. Mentoring is taking place within each group with some individuals using more than one colleague as mentors, in some cases using different people to act as mentors for different units.

Wherever possible assessment of individuals' evidence took place within the school with heads and deputies acting as internal assessors. In several schools, because of the small number of individuals involved, the internal assessor role was performed by a participant from another pilot school.

The external assessment function was provided by the project team, who analysed portfolios and gave individuals feedback on their evidence. During these sessions, the prime purpose was to explore consistency of interpretation and understanding of the standards. The aim was not to operationalize an accreditation scheme. It was recognized that an awarding body would normally train assessors and verifiers, approve centres and oversee unit certification.

Field testing the standards in schools

The intention of the pilot phase of the project was:

- to field test the SMS standards to see if they could be interpreted with adequate consistency and to develop effective systems of assessment; and
- to pilot the use of the standards as they relate to self-assessment (in preparation for appraisal) and team or institutional review. The emphasis was on management development rather than individual manager certification.

Details of the seven schools which participated in the field trials are shown in Table 1 overleaf.

Schools were informed about the many possible uses of the School Management Standards but all chose to use them either for self-assessment and/or school/team review. Use for self-assessment purposes could be in preparation for appraisal. The standards provided a framework for discussing an individual's contribution to the institution and acted as a guide for individuals in monitoring their own performance and establishing priorities for their further development.

The second intended use of the standards was to help evaluate and review the management practices and strategies within the school, and as a source of ideas for new policies on management development and

Table 1 *The pilot schools*

	School	Participants	LEA	Use of Standards 1 = self assessment 2 = sch/ team review
1	Primary (5-11)	Head, Deputy, Curric Co-ord	Croydon	1&2
2	Comprehensive (11-16)	Senior Management Team	Croydon	1&2
3	Special (4-18)	Head, Deputy, 3 x senior teachers	Berks	1&2
4	Comprehensive (11-18)	Deputy, 2 x Middle Managers	Berks	1
5	Infants (5-7)	Head, Deputy	Hants	1&2
6	Junior (8-11)	Head, Deputy	Hants	2
7	Comprehensive (11-18)	Deputy, 3 x middle managers	Bexley	1

training. In this way it was hoped that the standards could be used to improve the effectiveness of the organization and to help bring about any changes necessary for school improvement.

Most of the pilot schools decided to use a combination of self-assessment and school/team review. It was intended that each school or individual would be able to concentrate on the units which they perceived to be crucial for effective school management or which were seen as fundamental to the school's development. The aim was to build on existing developments and achieve compatibility with the school development plan. Although all units were covered by the schools, most individuals provided evidence for only one or two units. Some funds were made available to the schools and were used in most cases to provide supply cover. This cover enabled training or mentoring to take place. The schools were offered three days of introductory training before field testing the standards.

The experiences of the schools

In each school a senior member of staff, usually the headteacher, acted as project co-ordinator. Participants were given a clear brief. Their tasks were:

- to participate in the training;
- to compile and discuss evidence underpinning the competences;
- to attend meetings with project staff;
- to keep a record of the approximate time each individual had devoted to the pilot;
- to produce a short evaluation report and attend an evaluation conference.

Three basic questions were to be addressed in the evaluation report:

- Did the SMS standards make sense?
- Were there gaps or overlaps between the various units and elements?
- How easy had it been to gather evidence and assess competence?

Reflection on these questions was seen as valid learning and evidence which could be included in an individual's management portfolio.

An evaluation day took place when participants worked in small groups and gave consideration to:

- the content of the standards;
- the processes underpinning competence-based approaches; and
- other matters such as how schools can make best use of the standards.

As noted earlier each school was also asked to produce an evaluation report which was to cover these and other areas of interest.

Although not uncritical of the standards (especially the language) the schools did find that they helped individuals to produce their own personal development plans and to gain enlightenment about their own role in the school. The standards also helped people to understand each others roles and to gain insight into school management functions. For one school a competence-based system was 'a truly excellent way of approaching management development and is important in contributing to training and making training more systematic'.

The use of competence statements apparently forced individuals to reflect upon their role particularly with regard to practice and work performance. The collection of evidence and the identification of achievements was seen to be good for the self-esteem of the school manager and was said to help improve motivation and reduce stress. Four specific benefits for schools of using the standards were noted:

● professional working relationships are strengthened through the processes involved;
● they contribute to team building and help individuals to see where their job fits the whole;
● the standards provide a mechanism for the review of school management; and
● they will give the education sector credibility with other sectors – education management will be seen to be equally of worth compared with management in commerce and industry.

A competence-based approach to management development was seen as providing a useful framework to enable development to occur. It was not necessarily an alternative to other approaches to training and development but one of a number of possible instruments. It did have a number of advantages:

● it emphasizes workplace performance;
● establishes an infrastructure which encourages and enables development to take place;
● it is driven by practitioners rather than trainer providers;
● it allows for better identification of training and development needs;
● it provides a higher profile for career or personal development planning;
● it empowers and motivates individuals to use the standards in ways which reflect their own needs and those of the schools in which they work;
● it enables external inputs to be identified and tailored to an individual's or a school's development plan.

Conclusion

Later chapters will consider the wider national application of the SMS School Management Standards. It will be important to consider the SMS contribution to the enhancement of competence-based approaches to management development, training and accreditation for schools. The School Management Standards, the 'Guide to Evidence Collection and Assessment' and the Final Report of the School Management Competences Project raise many important issues in the national debate.

References

Earley, P., *The School Management Competences Project*, (Crawley School, Management South, 1992).

Jagger, J., 'Improving Competence', in *Managing Schools Today* (1991), 1, 4, 34-9.

Management Charter Initiative, *Assessment Guidelines*, (London: MCI, 1990).

Parsloe, E., *Coaching Mentoring and Assessing: a Practical Guide to Developing Competence*, (London: Kogan Page, 1992).

Part Three
Improving School Management

Chapter 9

Management Competence – Map or Mirage?

The competence movement – a sideways glance

In the preceding chapters you will have read about the positive response of teachers who have used competences to aid their own development as managers. The competence movement is gaining ground in schools. Movements can tend to develop disciples by conversion and there is always a danger of overstating the case for competence-based management development.

Management is not easily defined. Anyone who thinks that they can construct a DIY competence model to aid development in their school should read the 'health warnings' provided by some of the people closest to the competence movement.

Burgoyne (1989) has drawn attention to the elusiveness of a firm description of management when management has to define and create its own task. There are many 'right' ways of managing. Boyatzis (1982) summarizes our dilemma well: 'Management has been the focus of a great deal of study and commentary over the years. Some people profess to understand management through study, while others feel that it can only be understood through being a manager. What is a competent manager? Only years of systematic research may provide a comprehensive answer to that question, if it can be answered'.

There are many ways of trying to describe 'management'. Competence is not the only 'map' around. Management has been investigated in the context of other approaches: for example:

- the history of management;
- analysis of its functions;
- the natural language approach – what management means;
- the organizational theory standpoint from which management theories have been devised;
- cross-cultural comparisons of management in different countries; and
- empirical studies.

These and other approaches provide alternative means of mapping management.

The use of management competences is not universal in industry and commerce. Jacobs (1989) described an Ashridge survey of 500 organizations which underlined the surge of interest in the use of management competences. Nearly 70 per cent of private companies surveyed had some experience with competences. Several of these were at an early stage of developing competence-based programmes. A significant group of companies with experience had decided that competence-based programmes were not appropriate for their own particular needs. These were companies close to the high tech revolution. They had reorganized into 'loosely coupled and highly devolved businesses... They now believe that different parts of the company develop different values and ways of doing things that make it virtually impossible to address development needs in a single and uniform way'. In high tech companies the competence requirements may be situationally specific and vary over time. Individual needs also change. Jacobs reminds us that 'people perform successfully for different reasons, at different times and under different sets of circumstances'.

This does not deny the value of competence-based programmes in other situations. More traditional companies, including those sur-veyed during the development of the MCI Management Standards, found a generic competence framework helpful. It is important however that you do not leap on this bandwagon and become a disciple of the movement without a proper assessment of organizational and individual management development needs in your school. Before putting down this book and rushing off to seek an alternative to competence based management development it is important to look in more detail at the claims made for competence-based programmes by those who have used them.

The case for competence-based development

Management competences can provide you with a framework for analysing management requirements. They can also help you to identify training and development needs. 'One of the most important factors in developing management competence is likely to be awareness of own strengths and weaknesses in personal style of management and willingness to use that information in self development and adapting to the environment' (Schroder 1989). Those taking part in various pilot programmes in schools would support this view. Earley (1992) has outlined the benefits of the School Management standards reported by teachers. The standards:

- put the emphasis on workplace performance;
- help to establish an infrastructure that encourages and enables development to take place;
- are practitioner driven;
- assist better identification of training and development needs;
- provide a higher profile for career and development planning; and
- can empower and motivate individuals.

Teachers using the MCI Management Standards in the various projects described in earlier chapters would agree with these findings. MCI Management Standards have provided a useful framework for identifying the development needs of individual teachers and the school they work in. Individuals have also reported increased 'empowerment' as they have demonstrated management competences in the school. Some heads, hitherto reluncant to delegate some key management tasks, have been encouraged to do so.

These results are not unique to the MCI approach. Headteachers who have attended assessment centres testify to the usefulness of a competence framework. The claims then seem to support the use of competences whatever the model.

Competency in the context of human resource management

Competence based frameworks and programmes have to be seen however in the wider context of human resource development.

Burgoyne (1990) has pointed out that investment in management training does not correlate with improved corporate performance. There is evidence however that an integrated human resource management approach does correlate with performance.

Various elements of human resource management need to be integrated and related to corporate strategy in order to achieve a correlation with performance. There is a need to align career management and management development policy. The 'learning company' which is capable of developing itself and its workforce can use competences as a framework for good practice (Pedlar, Boydell and Burgoyne 1989). This has been implicit in much of the work done in the school based pilot schemes. Competences have been used for a variety of applications. Again, schools with a coherent management development policy and a clear understanding of their own aims and objectives have been best able to assist individual development.

Competences – one of several vehicles for management development?

The systematic development of competent managers has been about for some time. Everard (1990) reminds us that some alternatives have been well used and tested. Adair's Action Centred Leadership Model (ACL) has been widely used. Independent schools have used Industrial Society ACL courses to develop senior staff. I have also seen these courses used to good effect in the Lincolnshire LEA for the development of groups of primary headteachers. ACL courses concentrate on developing the skills that can be learned in achieving the task, building the team and developing the individual. I used this same model for developing skills for task, team and individual management as a training officer in the early 1960s so this approach has stood the test of time without reaching its 'sell by' date! Everard also reminds us that Coverdale training has also been widely used. 'It emphasizes the importance of skill and behaviour, rather than knowledge or personality, and shows how competent behaviour can be learned by carefully observing groups of people performing tasks, identifying and describing their successful practices and then planning to build on such success'. Many LEAs have used this approach.

As schools develop more autonomy, and as resources for management development become fragmented, the approaches described above may not be readily accessible to more than a handful of people, or at best, only to those who have already reached headship. A competence framework can be used in school to inform appraisal and other aspects of individual, team and whole staff development in the workplace. A competence framework can also inform and enhance other developmental approaches.

Developing management competences

Competence can be defined and categorized in many ways. It may be helpful to recognize that competence incorporates knowledge, skill, understanding and will (Burgoyne 1990). An individual manager is more than just a bag full of competences however. It is unrealistic to try to construct a complete picture of an individual with all their complexities. Indeed not every individual can be competent at everything. It is also essential to develop individual competences as part of an overall strategy to improve teams and the overall management capability of the organization.

Some basic skills are readily trainable: i.e. literacy, numeracy and basic analytical skills. You will have identified this level of specific skills in the various projects described. For example in the Oxford project written and oral communication skills are targeted.

It is possible to develop common general process skills. It is also possible to develop certain behavioural skills used in the process skills. Therefore an individual can be helped to develop the skills of chairing meetings and the behaviours which will enable them to exercise effective leadership of a group. Individuals can be helped to modify some behaviours and to strengthen their ability to work with other people.

Other competences are more elusive in developmental terms, for example the ability to learn, change and adapt as circumstances change. The skills of forecasting, anticipating and creating change are also more difficult to tackle. It is in these areas that planned experience in the workplace may be required over time, and even then there is no guarantee that an individual who has been unable to demonstrate these competences will do so given a wider field of responsibility in which to grow.

There is wide agreement, of course, about the personal competences that are desirable in managers. Sensitivity to the needs of others (or interpersonal search) appears in most competence models. It is very difficult to develop however. One of the most taxing jobs for an assessment centre director is to know what to say to the person who has demonstrated high organizational skills but who creates havoc through their inability to relate effectively to other people. It is likely that 'several important competences, including initiative, creativity, risk-taking and judgement, are unable to improve sufficiently to justify any sustained development activity' (Jacobs 1989).

Whatever model you are using, or proposing to use, it is essential to understand which competences can move beyond the diagnosis of development need to real development and change. Diagnosis is helpful as part of self assessment, career development planning and staff selection. For management development it is necessary to concentrate upon those competences that can be effectively developed.

Individuals and teams

There is increasing emphasis upon the careful selection and development of teams. Work on individual competences has moved away from the deficiency model of improving weaknesses (except for trainable skills) towards the building up of individual strengths to compensate for weaknesses. Selection of teams enables an organization to provide effective use of individuals. There is still a cultural expectation in this country that managers should be good at everything. If competences are to be used sensibly heads and governing bodies will have to come to terms with the scarcity of good all rounders and the fact that most managers are like the curate's egg, 'good in parts'.

Is there one preferred competence model?

There is one preferred model – and it is different for each group of competence enthusiasts! There is no simple solution. The MCI personal competence model has now been developed together with a description of the knowledge and understanding required of managers who will apply their competences in various contexts. Whilst being concerned with personal competences, the alternative models have also recognized the need to identify functional requirements in some detail where the training and development of skills and behaviours is concerned. The management standards seem to be concerned with outcomes and personal competence models with process. In various permutations both process and outcomes need to be considered.

119

It is necessary for you to consider the various options carefully. In the TVEI(E) Managing Coherence project (Isaacs 1992) the project team had to decide their approach to competences. They adopted several approaches to competence in their methodology. 'There has been the influence of functional analysis in providing the framework for our statements; yet the McBer approach has also influenced the programme.' This example shows that it is useful to find out as much as possible about the alternatives and then adopt a model which meets your requirements.

Developing a competence framework

There are distinct advantages in building upon the extensive development work undertaken by other people. The projects described in the earlier chapters probably fall into three categories:

Adoption – some schemes are adopting and applying the MCI Management Standards. Calderdale LEA, the College of Preceptors and Manchester Polytechnic (see Chapter Six and Chapter Seven) provide examples of this approach. The advantage is that the standards are spelt out in considerable detail. There is already a cadre of teachers who are familiar with the standards, having used them for development purposes. An important criticism of the standards is the 'alien' nature of the language. However some teachers have looked upon this as a challenge and say that they have benefited from trying to contextualize the generic standards in their own school.

Adaptation – the School Management Standards (Chapter Eight) are an example of adaptation of a model to a school context.The NEAC at Oxford (Chapter Four) has adapted the American NASSP standards in order to use them in the British context.

Improvement – some projects have involved an attempt to create a custom built scheme for the use of schools. These schemes are based upon a study of current models. The CEMD in the northwest and, the University of East London have built their own models with external help. The Cleveland headteachers have done the same (see Chapter Five).

The task of defining competence requirements for managers using the McBer approach demonstrates the care with which a competence model has to be constructed. David Fitt and Frank Hartle of the Hay Group (Fitt and Hartle 1992) recently outlined two approaches to this task. They have also contributed to a recent key work on competence-based human resource development (Mitrani, Dalziel and Fitt 1992).

The classical approach to defining competence requirements for managers requires the following steps:

- Define job accountabilities and performance measures;
- Understand main activities and tasks;
- Understand areas of difficulty and challenge;
- Nominate samples of 'outstanding' and 'average performers;
- Conduct behavioural event interviews with each;
- Analyse transcripts to identify common behavioural and attitudinal patterns and themes in each sample;
- Label behaviours and themes as competences;
- Present competences in 'clustered' or 'causal' model;
- Validate the competences.

This approach looks at the job as it is now. An alternative approach, attempts to take account of future as well as present requirements. This exercise has been done for headteacher competences by the Hay Group on behalf of a London borough. The steps in this projective approach are:

- Define future organization, strategy and values;
- Define the role(s) that will exist;
- Brainstorm challenges, difficulties and issues;
- Select competence requirements from a generic dictionary of competences;
- Provide behavioural indicators from selective behavioural event interviews.

The development of generic management standards also required a systematic approach, using functional analysis across a large number of organizations. A considerable volume of work was required of the researchers even before the standards could be piloted. The adaptation of those standards to produce the School Management Standards required further research.

There are already developed models which provide sufficient opportunity to test competence approaches in terms of their contribution to management development in schools. If a school or group of schools wish to develop their own model they should do so in collaboration with an expert partner who can provide specialist advice and resources.

Devising a model for use in school is not the end of the matter. It is necessary to consider how the model might be used and the requirements for internal school support for teachers using the model. Sources of external support also need to be identified and used.

Can competences be generic?

It is clear that there are a number of competences required in all situations, e.g. the ability to handle personal relationships sensitively. This still leaves the problem of the different requirements of organizations, some of which may still have traditional management hierarchies and others which require a more fluid and 'flatter' management structure.

Competences for different levels of management?

Competences required at different levels of management should be differentiated. This has been done in the Occupational Standards for Managers, but the work is yet to be completed at the senior managment level. The MI Standards appeal to junior managers because they provide a detailed agenda for development. Assisting the development of deputies who aspire to be heads is rather different. The projects working with head teachers see the personal competences of superior performers as a better basis for assessment and development.

Do competences last?

In all the schemes I have examined there seems to be an assumption that once a competence is gained it will never be lost. This is particularly worrying if managers are to receive accreditation in the form of an NVQ or some other formal recognition. If qualifications are based upon good evidence of performance in the workplace then there is a chance that skills can be securely grounded for future application in later jobs. However organizations, 'climate', the management style of leaders and external circumstances may change faster than the competence models. Is there a need for some kind of 'MOT test' for managers and for competence models?

Can everyone excel at everything?

The Occupational Standards for Managers require that accreditation is given for every element of competence if an NVQ is to be awarded. We have already seen however that people have strengths and weaknesses, and that some weaknesses are irretrievable. There must surely be a more realistic approach to accreditation. If not, even on management development programmes there will be a tendency for managers to try to get all the elements of competence ticked, even if, for some of them, they have only secured a simulation as the means of obtaining evidence of competence that is supposed to be valid for the whole of their professional life.

Different competences will come to the fore in different roles. Creativity may have little place in some closely defined management roles, yet it may have potential value once an individual proceeds to a different management role. Any competence model has to relate to the jobs people do and also to the jobs required they will do in the future.

Teachers often say that they are different. School managers spend much of their time managing people. The people competences are therefore more equal than other competences. This is exactly the point made by some organizations in the Ashridge study (Jacobs). Perhaps it is the competence research in bureaucratic and hierarchical organizations that is inappropriate for the newer forms of enterprise which are coping with constant turbulence and change. Yet even hierarchical bureaucracies need competent managers. What kind of organizations are schools? Are they domestic organizations obeying the regulations or wild ones fighting for their share of customers in the market?

School leadership competences – are they unique?

Current attempts to identify and apply competences in schools build upon a variety of initiatives and starting points. Are generic competences appropriate for schools? Should we be developing competences for schools as they are or as we desire them to be? Jenkins (1991) considers some of the current models to be rather old fashioned. He observes: 'if you had asked school leaders ten years ago if they would now be talking about creating a vision, the supremacy of the customer, getting rid of heirarchy and empowering staff, they may not have found it credible'. He goes on to suggest that schools have to become organizations which are designed to survive the constant pressure of an unpredictable and competitive environment. This new type of organization has been called 'post-entrepreneurial' because it brings entrepreneurial principles to the established corporation (Kanter 1989).

In this type of organization:

- bureaucratic processes are disappearing;
- reduction in levels of heirarchy are apparent;
- the differentiation between managers and workers is diminishing;
- cross-departmental collaboration is essential;
- segmentalism has broken down;
- staff are working in functional or cross-organizational teams;
- power has been handed down – individual staff and teams are empowered to act;
- open networks of information and negotiation replace heirarchical, top-down control of information;
- boundaries are breaking down within the organization between the organization and its customers and stakeholders;
- the organization is built around the contribution of skills of people, not on fixed roles.

However, there is still no single commercial or industrial model. Jacobs (1989) observes that the competence model works better for large bureaucratic organizations where business is stable and the environment predictable. Other enterprises have to live with uncertainty and find it more difficult to apply competence models. Cockerill (1989) has also distinguished between bureaucratic organizations where the emphasis is on planning, organizing and monitoring and organic structures, which gather new information and form ideas and well evaluated options. They have fluid networks and form teams across organizational boundaries. Managers must take, justify and be confident in the success of decisions when a 'right' solution does not exist. They must also get political support for decisions. Managers in organic organizations have to improve organizational performance in line with target dates.

Certainly Schroder's (1989) eleven high performance managerial competences aim to meet the requirements of a rapidly changing environment. Other models are available too. Morgan (1988) describes nine competences which meet the requirements of a changing environment. Dulewicz (1989) also describes twelve 'supra competences' that are quite close to the models described in Chapter Two.

Jenkins (1991) makes a plea for schools to adopt competences which incorporate a future view of managerial work rather than being locked into competence models which focus on past or present practice. He offers his own prescriptions to meet the needs of the school which will allow for a belief in vision, empowerment of staff, sensitivity to the needs of others, positive leadership and the need for constant change, development and improvement. He sees his prescriptions as reinforcing each other. All must be applied 'in the light of the vision of the organization'. The empowerment of staff and self-managing teams are key concepts that run through all the prescriptions.

Does competent management create effective schools?

How accurate is our view of the future tasks of school managers? Competent managers have to serve both current and future requirements. I participated in the OECD (Organization for Economic Co-operation and Development) Project on School Improvement during the mid 1980s. The project concluded that school organization and management were an essential component in the improvement of pupil learning.

More recently the school effectiveness movement has developed ideas about the present and future requirements of effective schools. Reynolds (1991) has proposed that the future agenda for research into school effectiveness will be complicated by the changed nature of leadership and management tasks in schools in the 1990s. Some of these changes are:

- a heightened public relations or marketing orientation and an ability to sell the product;
- the capacity to relate to parents;
- the capacity to find sources of support in the community;
- the capacity to manage rapid change, not to manage a steady state orientation;
- the capacity to motivate staff in times when instrumental rewards like promotion and advancement are rare;
- the capacity to relate to pupils, since the wave of future consumerism will...increasingly involve consumer opinion surveys with pupils.

The School Management Task Force summary of the characteristics of effective schools seems to be in tune with this prediction. Their analysis reflected HMI inspection evidence as well as other research work. The characteristics of effective schools are described in their report (ED/SMTF 1990) as follows:

- good leadership offering breadth of vision and the ability to motivate others;
- appropriate delegation with involvement in policy-making by staff other than the head;
- clearly established and purposeful staffing structures;
- well-qualified staff with an appropriate blend of experience and expertise;
- clear aims and associated objectives applied with care and consistency;
- effective communications and clear systems of record-keeping and assessment;
- the means to identify and develop pupils' particular strengths, promoting high expectations by both teachers and pupils;
- a coherent curriculum which considers pupils' experience as a whole and demonstrates concern for their development within society;
- a positive ethos: an orderly yet relaxed atmosphere of work;
- a suitable working environment;
- skills of deploying and managing material resources;
- good relationships with parents, the local community and sources of external support;
- the capacity to manage change, to solve problems and to develop organically.

This analysis of effective schools indicates that there is more to it than being able to manage change. Schools are not exactly like leading edge high-tech companies who have a rapidly changing environment. Much recent legislation has laid down detailed prescriptions for the National Curriculum, assessment and testing. The local management of schools and an the option to become grant maintained mean that school management has to take on board the strict requirements of effective financial planning, control and review. New skills of buying in services from the LEA or elsewhere require much more understanding of legislation and contract procedures. The requirements of record keeping, working with governors, providing a service to parents in accordance with the parents charter, staff appraisal and many other developments mean that schools have to become more effective as bureaucracies as well as being dynamic. The arrangements for school inspection will require other forms of effective record keeping and may also encourage the development of quality management systems in schools. All schools will have to display some of the characteristics of bureaucratic organizations simply because of the increased requirements to plan, organize and monitor what they are doing. The headteacher and his manager colleagues will have the dual demands of chief executive and leading professional. Both aspects of school management will have to be developed (Green 1992). School managers will have to display the competences required in bureaucratic organizations, yet at the same time to develop flatter hierarchies and increased use of the fluid networks and teams characteristic of newer forms of management. The new powers of governors will require headteachers to develop 'political' skills. It is curious that some of the prescriptions of the National Curriculum, e.g. the requirement to develop cross-curricular work, are likely to hasten the development of teamwork and other characteristics of non-bureaucratic organizations! School managers will need to display the characteristics of what Jay calls 'yogi' and 'commissar'.

Schools will be hybrid organizations – bureaucracies complying with national prescriptions, and dynamic organizations, recruiting pupils and seeking community support in a competitive quasi 'market'. A high priority will continue to be the management of people and their inter relationships.

One way in which schools are very different is that their product and workforce are the same. Pupils' learning is the main purpose of schools, yet, as pupils increasingly take responsibility for their own learning, they also become a workforce which manages the learning. Flexible learning approaches, the development of records of achievement and learning contracts, the change in the teacher's role towards that of enabler and tutor all make new demands of school management and increase the true management role of all teachers. Any competence model for schools has to cope with this special feature of their work.

The schools that have used or adapted the Occupational Standards for Managers have tried to cope with this by seeing management of pupils as part of the management of process or operations. More work is going to be needed here. Pupils are part of the workforce that manages learning. In this context, classroom management becomes a valid aspect of school management. Management of pupils as people as well as management of their learning as a process have to figure more prominently in future competence models. Because of these changes in schools competences could provide an effective framework for development. They are already being used to illuminate the development of the teacher's role in the management of pupil learning, for example, the Norfolk competence-based programme for teachers on the teaching of reading.

Conclusion

The changes that are taking place in schools are putting enormous pressures on school management. The ownership of a competence model, and its consistent use in all aspects of school management, can help schools to develop their capacity to manage what they have now and to assess their future management requirements. There is no one model that meets all needs. The functional analysis approach of the Occupational Standards for Managers and the School Management Standards has helped junior and middle managers to develop their skills. Once the problem of language is addressed teachers like the detailed prescriptions in that they provide a clear agenda for personal development. However, when it comes to the development of present and future senior managers the models based upon the characteristics of superior performers may be more appropriate. Schools do not have the time or the resources to undertake the fundamental research undertaken by some organizations. They have to draw upon the expertise that is there already and build new partnerships for competence-based management development.

References

Boyatzis, R. E., *The Competent Manager: a Model for Effective Performance*, (Chichester: John Wiley & Sons, 1982).

Burgoyne, J., paper to BEMAS Competences Workshop, Birmingham, March 1990, BEMAS Workshop Report 1990.

Burgoyne, J., 'Opinion' in *Transition* February 1989.

Cockerill, A., 'The Kind of Competence for Rapid Change', in *Personnel Management*, September 1989, pp.52-6.

Department of Education and Science, School Management Task Force, *Developing School Management: The Way Forward*, (London: HMSO, 1990).

Dulewicz, V., 'Assessment Centres as a Route to Competence', in *Personnel Management*, November 1989, pp.56-9.

Earley, P., 'Using Competences for School Management Development' School Management South/NFER paper to BEMAS Fourth Research Conference, University of Nottingham, 6-8 April 1992.

Everard, K. B., 'The Competence Approach to Management Development', in *Management in Education*, Vol. 4 No. 2, Summer 1990.

Fitt, D. and F. Hartle, 'Competencies in Education Management' paper to BEMAS Workshop, Woolley Hall, March 1992.

Green, H., 'Strategies for Management Development', in Stevens, D.B. (ed.) *Under New Management* (Harlow: Longman, 1991).

Isaacs, J., *TVEI(E) Managing Coherence 14-19* Four volumes, Bristol Polytechnic/Department of Employment 1992.

Jacobs, R., 'Getting the Measure of Competence', in *Personnel Management*, June 1989.

Jenkins, H. O., *Getting it Right: a Handbook for Successful School Leadership*, (Oxford: Blackwell, 1991), Chapter 11.

Kanter, R. M., *When Giants Learn to Dance* (London: Simon and Schuster, 1989).

Mitrani, A., M.M. Dalziel and D. Fitt, *Competence-Based Human Resource Management* (London: Kogan Page, 1992).

Morgan, G., *Riding the Waves of Change: Developing Managerial Competences for a Turbulent World* (San Francisco: Jossey Bass, 1988).

Pedlar, M., T. Boydell and J. Burgoyne, Towards the Learning Company, in *Management Development and Education*, Vol. 20/1, 1989.

Reynolds, D., 'School Effectiveness and School Improvement in the 1990s', International Conference on School Effectiveness Proceedings, Jerusalem, 1991.

Schroder, H. M., *Managerial Competence: the Key to Excellence* (Iowa: Kendall Hunt), 1989.

Chapter 10

Thirty or More Ways to Use a Competence Framework

Introduction

This Chapter provides some advice on how a competence framework might be used in schools. It also suggests ways in which you might use competences to assist management development. You have already learned that competences can bring 'empowerment' to teachers. Involvement with a competence framework is of little benefit if you do not intend to develop your own effectiveness and that of your school. To merely tick boxes on schedules in order to gain a qualification without achieving any real development is best described by a word accidentally thrown up by my word processor – *conpretence*!

The support of senior management is essential. Openness and a willingness to share ideas are essential. Some schemes allow for the fact that an individual teacher may be working in a hostile climate where prescription and 'mushroom management' prevail. In those cases external support is available. That solution is second best however. Benefits are greatest where the chosen competence model informs all aspects of human resource development in the school. Having said that, most people will want to start cautiously, test the model in an appropriate context in the school, and ensure that the work done is in tune with the school's mission, priorities and existing management development strategies. The wrong approach is to say 'here is a competence model I like, what can I use it for?' It is better to take stock first to see whether or not you or your school are ready for the demands that will arise from using competence as part of your development strategy.

There is a strong case for looking at what competence-based development can do for the whole organization as well as for the individual manager. The Calderdale LEA have considered this carefully. Their advice appeared in a recent article (Jagger 1992).

Jagger outlines how the MCI Standards might be used to support activity in four areas:

- in considering the organization and its structure and the individuals role within it;
- in recruitment to an organization;
- in establishing a precise tool for training needs analysis; and
- in quality control.

He suggests that comparing our organization with a generic structure allows us the opportunity to map our organization against an accepted model and to justify the variation. The exercise also takes us out of personal involvement and enables us to review the situation more objectively. A review of the organization against standards permits:

- analysis of the organizational and management structure at a time of stability;
- a set of reference points when seeking to establish why the existing structure might be failing; and
- an evaluative tool during periods of change within the structure.

The standards can help individuals to get an overview of their role and the role of others within the organization. Familiarity with the standards:

- helps to clarify roles and brings meaning to job descriptions through analysis and description of the management activity expected;
- allows individuals and teams to relate their management activity to that of others and the organization as a whole;
- encourages recognition of shared or inter-relating activity with others in the organization (or other organizations) and reduces the sense of isolation;
- makes the clarification of roles in team delivery easier where a shared language and ready made functional analysis is available.

It is important to ensure that any model is capable of helping to develop the management capability of the school staff as a whole. Nevertheless you may decide to start small and pilot a model with individual managers or with a team.

A menu of options

The MCI Occupational Standards for Managers and the Personal Competences Model have a number of suggested applications. These are outlined in Chapter Three. The School Management Standards (see Chapter Eight) also have some suggested applications.

Individual, team and whole school review and development can benefit from the use of a competence framework not least because it provides a common frame of reference and structure for development.

Individual development

A competence framework can be of considerable benefit to the individual manager. There are various steps required for the effective development of competences. These have been described (Everard and Morris 1990) as follows:

- recognition of the various elements or units of competence;
- understanding their nature and how they relate to managerial effectiveness;
- self assessment or other feedback (such as appraisal) on the level of competence;
- experimentation with displaying the competence, or demonstrating it at a higher level of effectiveness, with systematic feedback; and
- continuous concious practice in using the competence;
- applying it along with other relevant competences as an integral whole, in a range of work situations.

Individuals need considerable support at the outset, in order to understand the competence model used. This can be provided by an external agency or by experienced colleagues in the school already familiar with the model.

Perhaps the most powerful instrument for individual development is the portfolio. This provides a means of organizing the record of a manager's development.

Two examples of the use of portfolios

1. *The College of Preceptors – candidate's portfolio of evidence*

The portfolio is a vehicle for development as well as a record of achievement. The individual can record and present evidence, both current and prior, on individual development, personal competence and functional competence at work. This provides a means of integrating theory and practice in the development programme. The portfolio is a useful focus for looking back at past achievements and looking forward to future personal and professional development. It is 'housed' in an A4 ring binder and is built up step by step. It will include:

- a summary of the individual's previous professional experience and a copy of their current job description;
- the ACP record book which gives details of the requirements for each element of competence, including examples of the type of evidence required;
- a summary of short term and longer term development needs based upon a personal assessment of strengths and areas for improvement. This is completed with the help of another colleague in the workplace;
- a record of the priorities for the candidate's work on the ACP programme, taking account of individual and school development priorities;

The portfolio will include evidence of prior learning or experience; 'hard' evidence such as reports, plans and minutes of meetings; 'soft' evidence which is more subjective and might include appraisal from line managers or peers, self assessment of progress in meeting development goals and statements from other people with knowledge of the candidate's work. This might involve governors, people from the local community or teachers from other schools with whom the candidate may have a formal work link.

In this case the portfolio is used as the basis for formal assessment with a view to obtaining accreditation. The portfolio approach is still evolving. On the current pilot schemes candidates' portfolios are now expected to include action plans and contract learning documents as well as examples of reflective self analysis.

It is important that people are honest with each other and with themselves. As one Norfolk ACP candidate has said: 'Write it as it is, not as you would like it to be, nor as you think it should be'. The Norfolk candidates are advised that the portfolio can also help to foster a creative interaction between the participant and the self-development process that is taking place; between the participant and others taking part who are also in the process of self-development and between the participant and the facilitators whose role it is to foster such self-development.

2. *Personal management portfolio – School Management South*

This second example of a portfolio (Knight and Close 1992) is not tied to a particular development programme, but is devised for use by individual school managers for their own self development. It is described as 'an experiential approach to learning about management'. The portfolio has three units entitled: 'Refections on Experience'; 'Personal Management Profiles' and 'The Cjreer Development Profile'. Duplicates of some pages are provided for photocopying. The portfolio has been specifically designed to allow teachers who have taken on new management roles to conduct review and mapping exercises alongside their own daily work. It is designed 'to help you to record your daily management experience in usable, tangible form; recognize, analyse and reconstruct the knowledge to be gained from that experience and make use of that knowledge for the purpose of your own further development as a manager'. Two competence models are offered as alternative frameworks for review. One is the School Management Standards developed by School Management South (see Chapter Eight) and the other is the personal competences model for middle managers devised by the Cleveland Heads group whose work is described in Chapter Five.

Considerable experience was gained in the profiling projects funded by the School Management Task Force. For example the Consortium for Education Management Development (see Chapter Five) provided a 'Profile of Management Development' which included particular exercises for individuals to use in self review. This started with an individual reviewing a recent management activity, writing an evaluation of it, discussing it with a 'critical friend' and summarizing their commments in writing using personal evaluation forms provided in a ring binder of profiling materials.

Management competence and appraisal

Appraisal is a mandatory means of nurturing self development available to every school. It is another means of promoting management development which might be enhanced by the use of a competence model. The Cleveland Heads' Group (see Chapter Five) have explored the use of competences to aid the self appraisal and classroom or task observation stages of the appraisal cycle. The group has developed materials for appraisal, including two booklets which provide advice and documentation for self appraisal. The task of the individual is to compare actual and ideal profiles for each competence. In the first part of the exercise individuals rate the importance of each behaviour in terms of importance to their job. They are then asked to rate how effectively they perceive themselves demonstrating each behaviour. The resulting profile serves to assess the degree to which an individual demonstrates the thoughts, feelings and behaviour associated with school based middle management – 'the actual'. It also assesses the 'should be', i.e. the degree to which an individual expects himself or herself to demonstrate these competences for excellent performance in the job.

A Headteacher or other colleague, possibly the appraiser, can also complete the same exercise. Disagreements can be discussed. These may arise from the inability of the participant to assess themselves accurately. For example, some people underestimate their own capabilities, or appraiser and appraisee may not get on together and this might affect responses. In other cases a colleague may not have sufficient information to make an accurate assessment. In all cases the competence approach forces differences and difficulties into the open and promotes a more honest review of individual performance and development.

This exercise and the discussion based upon it can then help the individual to prepare for the appraisal dialogue. It may also suggest priorities for classroom or task observation. The exercise can also inform the appraisal dialogue and help to determine development targets.

The Cleveland team is continuing to trial and develop these materials.

There are alternative approaches that can be tried, for example an analysis of what the individual manager likes or dislikes doing may provide a useful guide to development needs.

In some companies the use of the competence framework in appraisal has been further developed to identify those competences which might contribute specifically to the objectives for the year ahead.

It must be remembered however that individual managers learn in different ways and in the context of appraisal, there should be some flexibility provided where optional additional materials and exercises are available.

Whole school and team review and development

It is the experience of the teachers on the various pilot projects, that individual review, based on competence, triggers review and development in the team and in the school. This is partly because competence models are capable of providing a framework for critical review of current performance. It is not long before an individual who has studied the performance requirements realizes that their own performance can be enhanced as can that of other colleagues. The people supporting individual development, heads, mentors or other peers, have also seen the relevance of the individual's work to the development of the institution. Here are two specific examples:

A middle manager in a secondary school undertook a survey among her colleagues as part of her review of her own performance in managing people. Her questionnaire to midday supervisors and school meals staff revealed considerable relationships problems with another colleague, arising, mainly, from inadequate school guidelines and policies for supervision. This was discussed with the colleague concerned and then, by mutual agreement, with the head. The ACP candidate was then given the task of devising new policy and procedures. This was done, and a follow up questionnaire and discussion with supervisory staff marked a significant improvement in morale and inter-personal relationships.

The head of a primary school supported a teacher in their school who was participating in the ACP programme. The individual required experience of making a presentation to other people. The head arranged for a presentation to governors which was well received. His purpose was twofold: to help the development of the individual, and to encourage the governors to invite members of staff to their meetings to discuss the schools needs and achievements. The work of the individual candidate in this case has resulted in considerable governor interest in staff development and a desire to hear more about the work of the school at their regular meetings.

School review

The Calderdale local education authority is about to use the Occupational Standards for Managers to support the preparation of job descriptions and other aspects of developing a new management structure in a school which is the result of amalgamation between two former schools.

Competence models provide a useful framework for reviewing the school. This kind of exercise is enhanced where there is a clear schedule of the detailed requirements of management in terms of process and outcomes. An interesting example of such a schedule arose from the work of the TVEI(E) Managing Coherence 14-19 programme. The Bristol Polytechnic team devised the schedule as a result of their own work in Dudley, Dorset and Wiltshire schools and on the work of other associated project teams, particularly that of Sheffield Polytechnic on monitoring, evaluation and review. The full schedule is included in their final report (Isaacs 1992).This schedule has drawn on the Occupational Standards for Managers and on the McBer personal competences. The result is a very comprehensive schedule for departmental, faculty, team, or whole school review. It assists a thorough audit of current and desired management behaviours and outcomes. Statements of functions, tasks and skills cover the following areas:

- Manage the environment;
- Manage resources;
- Manage people;
- Manage information systems;
- Manage internal change;
- Manage the curriculum

- Manage progression; and
- Personal effectiveness.

Team development

Individuals are usually keen to use competence for their own self development. Developing team members together requires great sensitivity. It is usually necessary to remind team members that competences provide a structure for progressively improving the capabilities that people already possess. In the context of team building this focuses upon team leadership and team membership competences. The aim is not to make fundamental changes in people. Team review may involve:

- improvement of the team in achieving its task;
- improvement of the process by which it achieves its task, including positive interpersonal behaviours; and
- the enhancement of individual development through team membership.

Competence models can also aid the choice of teams, based not upon status, but skills. The development of flatter hierarchies, team management of institutions and the increasing use of temporary task groups will be enhanced if there is a clearer view of people's strengths. Teams as well as individuals can benefit from the production of portfolios. A team portfolio format could aid team development. Collaborative action research is already accepted for accreditation by some higher education institutions. All the better if the collaboration is focused upon the enhancement of the team leading to greater efficiency in achieving objectives and greater effectiveness as a working group.

Staff selection

The Educational Assessment Centre initiatives have made management development their main focus. It has not been long however before some LEAs, governors and heads have sought to use the centres to inform selection procedures. This has been the main use of centres in the USA and is becoming an important part of the work of centres in this country. Attempts are being made to develop selection packages that are phase specific and that may also provide feedback on those competences that the client school considers to be most important. The pragmatic British approach is therefore less of a blunderbuss and is better targeted at specific competences. Generally, a profile is provided for a list of candidates. No suggested rank order or 'winner' is provided to the potential employer. The assessment centre information provides added value to the total information available to the appointing body. One of the client LEAs of the NEAC project (Chapter Four) is planning to put all those aspiring to primary headship through an assessment centre some time before promotion. This will aid individual development and LEA succession planning.

It is difficult to see how far assessment centres will develop this work. Ideally, every teacher on the promotion ladder should have a management portfolio which gives a full account of the individual's experience, career progression and competence. This would include a report from an assessment centre and other developmental and training activities undertaken outside the school. Were such a portfolio available there could be a considerable enhancement to selection procedures.

Some companies have found that familiarity with the assessment centre criteria and process can help interviewers to be more objective about each candidate's credentials and ready to compromise on the 'ideal'. A shared understanding of competence and its language might also help people to give honest and helpful feedback to unsuccessful candidates for promotion. However a report from an assessment centre in the hands of an unskilled and ill informed interviewer has its cutting edge severely blunted, and great damage can be done.

Selection must be part of a coherent management development policy. The use of competence in selection procedures makes most sense where the other aspects of human resource development in a school are also informed by a competence framework.

Support for competence-based development

The main responsibility for helping teachers to develop management competency must rest with the school. In the words of the School Management Task Force: 'The school must take the main responsibility for developing its own capacity to manage' (SMTF 1990). This is less easy in the two or three teacher school where the head has a full teaching timetable. It may be easier in the large secondary school. Whatever the size of the school some initial help may be required. An external agency – higher education course provider, local education authority, industrial or commercial enterprise or an individual consultant can help you to grapple with some of the basic problems inherent in competence-based management development. You may require:

1. Help with choosing and devising a competence framework. There are now a number of 'off the peg' models available. It is therefore relatively easy to obtain information and support from individuals, schools and providing bodies who have used or developed well established competence models. Providers can also offer competence based management development programmes for use by individuals or groups. These will usually carry some form of accreditation. If you want to have a model tailored to your own context then some outside expertise will be needed. You will require realistic advice on the advantages and lir .tations of your scheme. It is important for the users of any scheme to be aware of the limitations of an approach. Evidence of a manager's competence may not be easy to assess objectively and every scheme must have an element of subjective judgement within it.

2. Assistance with overcoming the unfamiliarity of the language of competence. Some people argue that the competences, behaviours, desired outcomes and performance criteria should be translated into a language familiar to teachers. Some of the schemes reviewed have done this, either by redefining a competence model or by providing explanatory notes for teachers. Some have gone further and have prepared materials for use in school which contextualize competences not only in terms of definitions and descriptions, but in terms of how they relate to the management tasks familiar to teachers in their day to day work. Some teachers take a different view of the language problem. They believe that having to grapple with the language of competency and contextualize it for yourself is a valuable development exercise in itself. This exercise still needs advice from someone familiar with the particular competence model to ensure that you have not mistranslated definitions, behaviours or performance criteria.

3. Help with assessment of competence. Effective assessment requires people to be honest and open with each other and with themselves. Individuals tend to be hard on themselves and to misjudge their own competence. Managers need a critical friend who will help them come

to a balanced assessment of their competence. An outside source of help and advice can assist you to make balanced assessments of competence.

4. Help with understanding the nature of evidence of competence. Evidence can be derived from many sources: performance at work, specially set assignments, simulations, 'witness testimony' from your own reflection on practice, and the testimony of peers, your boss, or members of the wider community with whom you work. Detailed advice on how to produce and assess good evidence is available.

5. Help with effective use of accreditation. Teachers are motivated by accreditation of work done to develop their management competence. There is a problem here. It is all too easy to fall into the temptation of letting the accreditation tail wag the development dog; 'The last temptation is the greatest treason, to do the right deed for the wrong reason' (Eliot 1935). Accreditation schemes can encourage people to tick boxes and short circuit the hard work required to achieve real development. Schemes will allow for accreditation of prior learning or achievement. An important aspect of your self development is the assessment of this prior achievement. A 'critical friend, perhaps a colleague in school', can be of help here. The task of recognizing where you are in terms of attainments, skills, knowledge and abilities needs support. Assessment of prior achievement is no soft option. A supporting tutor can help to:

- identify what an individual knows and can do;
- equate those skills and knowledge with specific competence requirements;
- assess the individual against the competences, standards or performance criteria; and
- agree the 'credit' that the learner can claim for competences already attained (Simosko 1991)

There are many other support requirements. Assessment of prior achievement is only part of the process. Although the portfolio, self study materials and wise colleagues in the workplace should provide most of the support required, it may be necessary to fill gaps in support with outside help.

6. Help with opportunities to develop competences. Individuals need to try out new behaviours. They also need to practice competences in

their daily work. Much can be done in the school to give people broader management experience. However different competences may be developed in different ways. A simple example of a trainable skill is time management, a part of the competence to plan and organize work. An individual could use self study materials or attend an external time management course.

Conclusion

In order to benefit from the introduction and use of competence based management development it is necessary to review your aims and your existing starting point:

- What is the current state of management and management development in your school? Are you ready to empower people? Do you have a clear institutional development policy, a policy for human resource development, appropriate management structures that support your educational aims and an open supportive development 'climate'?
- Do you have a preferred competence model in mind?
- Have you assessed the degree to which your school is capable of introducing competence based management development?
- Have you worked out the external help that you will require?
- Is there an action plan and is it realistic?

The current state of management in your school is the key. It may be that a competence model will be needed in order to give you a framework for your initial 'well school' clinical review. The next chapter looks at some of the features of effective support. It may help you to decide how much you can do for yourself at this stage. The ultimate target is to develop the capacity of the school, and all the individuals in it, so that they can manage their own development, and ultimately be better managers.

References

Department of Education and Science, School Management Task Force, *Management Development in Schools: the Way Forward*, (London: HMSO, 1990).

Eliot, T. S., *Murder in the Cathedral*, (Faber, 1935).

Everard, K. B., and G. Morris, *Effective School Management* 2nd edition, (London: Paul Chapman Publishing, 1990).

Isaacs, J., TVEI(E), *Managing Coherence 14-19*, (Bristol Polytechnic/ Department of Employment, 1992).

Jagger, J., The Use of the MCI Standards as a Development Tool, in *Mentor*, Autumn?1992.

Knight, J., and A. Close, *The Personal Management Portfolio: An experimental approach to learning about management*, (School Management South, 1992).

Simosko, S., *APL: A Practical; Guide for Professionals*, (London: Kogan Page, 1991).

Chapter 11

Supporting the Self-managing School

Support services have the task of empowering individuals and schools. The aim is to ensure that each school develops a positive 'climate' which encourages individual and institutional development, and therefore better teaching and learning. It is also vital to give each school the capacity to manage that development effectively.

The self managing and self developing school will benefit however from outside services from time to time.

Local education authorities and LEA consortia currently provide documentation, information about sources of help, training opportunities, advisory support, networking and other forms of support. In developing the use of competences you should check what is already available to you through the LEA or other external support system (e.g. the Grant Maintained Schools Centre). Various aspects of support have to be considered. Some of these may be already available in your school, or may be developing. Others will be available from external sources.

Mentoring

'Self development is rarely successful without the support of other people – providing individuals with someone who can give feedback, question, share, discuss, challenge, comfort and guide one through the learning and development cycle' (Kirkham 1992).

The NEAC at Oxford has developed a network of mentors to work with protégés who have participated in an assessment centre. It is their view that your own head or other colleagues in school may be able to handle coaching in skills at work, but a critical friend external to the school can help you with your personal development plan (Green, Holmes and Shaw 1992). This model of external mentoring can be of help to individuals, including those who have less positive support in their school. The focus is not upon the practical management of the school or personal and private matters but upon individual professional development. The external mentor could be well placed to advise a manger who has real difficulties or false expectations of promotion prospects.

The mentor has been defined as a wise and trusted guide, advising, not telling; mentoring not protecting; a resource and not a clinical counsellor; and supporting rather than building false expectations (Simosko 1991).

Many other schemes use in house mentors. They have an important role in negotiating work assignments, counselling, supporting candidates and helping them to produce realistic action plans (CNAA/BTEC 1990). The ACP (Management) programmes have used mentors in this way. The mentor has helped to negotiate and plan work assignments which extend the individual's opportunities to demonstrate management competences. The School Management Standards project had one school where group mentoring had been undertaken in house with considerable success. Group mentoring could also work well in the case of a cluster of small schools. Whatever the approach adopted the selection of mentor is crucial. They require both sufficient management experience and credibility and the ability to support and encourage without becoming directive. Good mentors are part of the infrastructure that enables individuals and teams to develop through their own effort. Training to be a mentor provides other managers with development opportunities too.

Coaching

This task should be undertaken in the workplace. It requires regular contact, and is a natural part of the work of a line manager such as a head of department. The focus is upon skills and competences in action, feedback on performance and accountability. In the Cheshire Education Management Programme a pilot group of secondary schools are about to trial the use of a competency model produced originally in Cheshire for colleges of further education (FEU 198-). The individual manager follows a programme of self assessment and review with a line manager. Continuous development follows, with the line manager's help. Some external seminars are provided on the areas covered in the competence profile.

Assessing

Effective assessment is essential. It is also a difficult task to undertake whether self assessment or the assessment of other people. Many of the schemes described have recruited assessors who are experienced managers and who have a thorough understanding of school management. Assessors working in assessment centres have high physical and mental demands put upon them. This has been confirmed by the 'witness testimony' of assessors and participants at assessment centres! Many of these assessors have been initially self selected and are highly motivated people. Assessors need careful preparation and training in order to assess workplace evidence or assessment centre exercises. Assessors should be able to give clear advice to others on what constitutes good evidence of competence.

Tutoring

The programmes carrying accreditation provide some external tutor support. This support is much less intensive than on a traditional academic programme. The tutor is responsible for a small group of candidates, may arrange occasional meetings, and will encourage candidates to provide a self supporting network. The tutor will be on call, either at regular 'surgery' sessions or over the telephone to provide advice. For example, on the ACP (Management) programmes the tutor is expected to help the candidate to:

- understand the guidelines and the Occupational Standards for Managers;
- plan the portfolio of evidence;
- review the outcomes of past experience to determine evidence of existing competences;
- undertake an analysis of personal and professional development needs, using the standards;

- determine ways in which the individual's current work at school might be used to develop and assess competences;
- select relevant reading, including self-study materials;
- negotiate suitable work assignments, where this cannot be done by the candidate's school based mentor.

The tutor may also act as an assessor for another group of candidates.

All of these duties could, ultimately be undertaken by senior managers in schools. There is still need, however, to build up a cadre of people in schools who are familiar with the use of competency frameworks. Schools already have people with excellent mentoring, assessing and counselling skills and it may only be a matter of time before larger schools in particular, begin to provide their own tutors.

Supporting trainers and developers

External bodies can help the school to build up its own expertise. For example, the Training and Development Lead Body (TDLB) has set National Standards for Training and Development. These provide a useful framework for the development of various categories of support staff. The National Standards address the following areas:

- Identify training and development needs;
- Design training and development strategies and plans;
- Provide learning opportunities and support;
- Evaluate the effectiveness of training and development; and
- Support training and development advances and practice.

All of these areas are part of the overall purpose of the standards to 'develop human potential to assist organisations and individuals to achieve their objectives'.

The Standards for Assessment and Verification (TDLB 1991) which are part of evaluating the effectiveness of training and development, can help the 'front line' assessor. The line manager or colleague responsible for professional development in the school can learn to develop assessor skills. Similarly the people who support the assessment work in schools can also learn to co-ordinate and verify the assessment process. The main units in the standards are:

- Design systems for the collection of evidence;

- Assess candidate performance;
- Assess candidate using diverse evidence;
- Co-ordinate the assessment process;
- Verify the assessment process; and
- Identify previously acquired competence.

Training for mentors and assessors is provided by some organizations in the context of their own schemes. Those using the Occupational Standards for Managers or the School Management Standards are likely to use the TDLB Standards mentioned above. The assessment centre providers already train their own assessors and mentors. The Cleveland project has the advantage of support from a major industrial enterprise which uses the same approach to competence and has provided specific training and advice. The NEAC at Oxford provide two days of training for mentors. This includes a menu of models and skills and introduction to a code of practice for mentors. There is also an emerging network for mentors who can give each other support and advice.

Providing support materials

There is a growing availability of support materials for schools wishing to use a competence approach. The materials include:

- Information about competence models, e.g. the Occupational Standards for Managers and the School Management Standards.
- Information about the competence model with further advice on competence development. One example of this is the 'Competences' booklet produced for Cleveland teachers by the Cleveland/ICI Heads' Group (1992). This booklet is designed as a working document to provide guidance for individuals who wish to develop any competence. It can be used by individuals themselves or with their managers. The purpose of the booklet is help performance improvement. Ideas, suggestions and learning strategies to develop the 14 competences form the basis of the booklet. Users are invited to add to the booklet. For each competence the booklet lists behavioural indicators, self-development activities and manager's support activities. This is in the category of what one manager described as 'a cookbook of diagnostic tools and practical therapies' (Glaze 1989).
- Specific advice on various aspects of a scheme. For example the Occupational Standards for Managers are supported by other MCI

documentation on matters such as portfolios, underpinning knowledge and understanding and assessment.

- A framework listing the competences that are required for management of an institution such as the TVEI(E) material described in Chapter Ten (Isaacs 1992).
- Ready made portfolio materials or advice on portfolio preparation.
- Competence development has to be seen in the total context of management development. There are many good self-study materials available to school managers. Some of these could usefully be indexed for use with competence models. This strategy is being planned by the College of Preceptors at present. It is also likely that new self study materials on management, for example those from the Open University, will be capable of cross referencing to one or more competence models.
- A schedule of training and development opportunities, related to the competence model, for example the one being developed by the NEAC at Oxford.

Centres providing support for competence development are building up 'banks' of materials for supporting the development of management competence in schools. In some cases self-study materials will be available on loan to individuals or schools.

Supporting networks

All of the main projects have emphasized the importance of providing opportunities for participants, assessors and mentors to meet to exchange ideas. In some instances groups of schools have begun to work together in the same way. There is a need for isolated individual school managers to meet colleagues. Sharing of information and working together to prepare portfolios, or to improve assessor or mentor skills are a vital aspect of support. This can be arranged by the LEA, the institution supporting a competence-based programme or by schools themselves who decide to initiate a scheme of their own, using a common competence model. Collaboration between schools provides an opportunity to share expertise and provide wider experience for managers on a development programme.

Assessment centres and development workshops

Assessment centres

Assessment centres have a valuable role to play in support of individual development. The basic criteria for assessment centres are:

- the use of multiple assessment techniques, of which at least one must be a simulation;
- more than one assessor, all rigorously trained to exacting standards;
- the centre must attempt to simulate key components of the job in question;
- judgement must be based on pooling information for all assessors and all assessment techniques;
- this overall evaluation of behaviour must take place at a separate time from observation of behaviours during the exercises (Lyons and Jirasinghe 1992).

Assessment centres provide identification of an individual's management competences, assessment of performance, feedback and suggestions for further development. They can also provide help to individuals after attendance at a centre by means of mentoring and other support. There is considerable discussion of the timing when attendance at an assessment centre might be most beneficial. This timing may be determined by employers who each have a particular strategy in mind. They may see the assessment centre as a means of assisting the development of potential heads. Others use the centre to stimulate the further induction and development of newly appointed heads. Providing heads with the opportunity of being an assessor at a centre can be another valuable development opportunity.

If centres are used it is vital that their contribution is seen in the context of an individual's development generally. The evaluation of the Oxford Assessment Centre (Esp and Young 1991) recommended that there should be clear information provided to the centre by the individual and their current employer. Individuals coming to the centre may have already considerable prior opportunities for development. If a centre is to make recommendations for further development, its staff need to know this, and also to be aware of forward plans for that same individual's development. As the use of personal management portfolios develops this must become an integral part of the work of assessment centres.

In the USA it is not uncommon for teachers to pay for their own attendance at a centre. It remains to be seen whether or not any individuals will do the same thing in the UK. At present it is only possible to claim tax relief where a training or development opportunity leads to a National Vocational Qualification.

Development workshops

These are used in industry to provide opportunities for developing specific competencies. Schools will benefit from this kind of opportunity. Existing providers deal with this in various ways. They may provide workshops which fill gaps in the experience and knowledge of individuals. For example, junior managers will have little knowledge of personnel procedures and a short session can familiarize them with the principles and practices of interviewing, disciplinary or grievance procedures. Larger schools should be able to provide this support for their own staff, but many teachers will need opportunities of this kind to be provided by the LEA or other external provider. The NEAC at Oxford has provided workshops on the subject of values in education. Value systems are there behind every competence model and it is vital that this aspect of competence work is further developed.

Conclusion

This Chapter has looked at some of the ways in which external sources can support development in schools. Local education authorities already have advice on their general support systems for management development (SMTF 1990). They are exhorted to have a policy, an organizational structure and a schedule for developing that policy. Further, they are recommended to have a team of officers and advisers with resources and expertise to provide management services to schols. Their range of non-training support services might include:

- easily accessible management information services;
- technical advice;
- support for collaborative peer-group action, inter-school development projects and study groups;
- information about the location, of other advice and support available to schools;

- identification of reliable consultants and mentors; and
- an advisory service to help teachers plan their career in education.

Local education authorities have taken many initiatives already in support of competence based management development in schools. However, the current and proposed changes in their role raise questions about the viability of the support structure. No major company would leave its human resource development policies, strategies and implementation to a variety of providers, scattered unevenly across the land. Twenty four thousand schools and their many managers and potential managers deserve better than that.

Support is already available from higher education institutions, professional associations and private consultants. They, as well as LEAs will have to have a clear understanding of the various types of support required by self-managing schools. This will not be provided as easily in the future. There will be need for a clear specification of the support required.

Chapter Twelve looks at the support entitlement that should be provided at national level and the arrangements for monitoring the development of management in schools.

References

CNAA/BTEC, *The Assessment of Management Competences*, (CNAA/DE (training), 1990).

Esp, D., and M. Young, *Stage 1 Evaluation Report*, to the Director of the NEAC, (July 1991).

Glaze, Tony, 'Cadbury's Dictionary of Competence', in *Personnel Management*, July 1989.

Green, H., G. Holmes, and M. Shaw, *Assessment and Mentoring for Headship*, (Oxford: School of Education Oxford Polytechnic, 1991).

Isaacs, J., TVEI(E), *Managing Coherence 14-19*, (Bristol Polytechnic/Department of Employment, 1992).

Kirkham, D., in M. Wilkin (ed) *Mentoring in Schools*, (London: Kogan Page, 1992).

Lyons, G., and D. Jirasinghe, research paper, (1992).

Simosko, S., *APL: The Accreditation of Prior Learning*, (London: Kogan Page, 1991).

Training and Development Lead Body, *National Standards for Training and Development Supplement, Aug. 1991, Standards for Assessment and Development*, (London: HMSO, 1991).

Chapter 12

School Management Competence – a National Priority?

A national system of support?

The United Kingdom has been applauded by some American observers for its national effort to establish occupational standards and national vocational qualifications. Part of that effort has been the development of generic Occupational Standards for Managers. In addition the Department of Employment has assisted a number of projects including the School Management Standards project and the Oxford National Educational Assessment Centre. The Department of Education and Science (now the Department for Education) funded the first evaluation of the Oxford project and has also funded research work on values and a number of profiling projects which have included some use of competence based frameworks. The School Management Task Force also examined and tested the use of self study materials for management development in schools.

However the School Management Task Force has completed its work and has gone. The local education authority consortia remain as do funds for management training and development. But how far did the Task Force achieve their remit to:

- work with the public and private sector providers to ensure that adequate provision is available;

- help local authorities to establish practicable strategies for ensuring adequate management development and training for heads and senior staff in schools; and
- assist local education authorities to set quantified targets for achievement of management training of their existing heads and senior staff over a given time period (DES/SMTF 1990).

The Task Force, and other initiatives have certainly added to the capacity for schools to manage themselves but the situation on the ground seems as patchy as it has ever been. Some local education authorities have been more active than others but a coherent management development programme for all school managers is still to be achieved.

Future plans for increased local management of schools and a large number of grant mantained schools leave open the question of who will co-ordinate and provide support for school management development. To leave everything to 24,000 separate institutions without the benefit of clear advice and support is not satisfactory. Local education authorities may survive for some time, but they will be increasingly hard pressed to provide the volume and range of support for school management that the most active authorities have achieved hitherto. Schools will have the choice of buying services from local authority established trading units or from other providers. There is no guarantee however that there will be accessible support across the country. The new funding councils have yet to show the degree to which they will be concerned with school management, beyond their obvious concern that budgets should be balanced and funds spent in accordance with the Audit Commission's three 'E's of economy, efficiency and effectiveness. It is possible to live with several sources of support and advice within a national framework but there seems to be no guarantee of effective support for all schools.

Later in this Chapter you are invited to consider what, if any, the role of national government should be with regard to supporting competence based management development in schools. First of all it is necessary to ask whether competence is that important and if so, whether it can be best managed as near to the schools as possible without directives from the Secretary of State.

Are competence-based developments helpful?

The verdict of teachers who have tried them is 'yes', with the usual reservations about unfamiliarity of language, other pressures of day to day work and an overload of initiatives in school. The development of managerial competence has to start in the workplace. 'One of the most important factors in developing managerial competence is likely to be awareness of own strengths and weaknesses in personal style of management and willingness to use that information in self development and adapting to the environment' (Schroder 1989). The 'witness testimony' of many teachers is that competences enable self review and development to be practitioner driven. A competence framework provides career development and training and development provision with a framework and a credible rationale based upon job performance. Competence models cannot descibe the whole person, but they do have the capacity to help people to improve as managers, and in the process to be better motivated. Another experience of many teachers is the willingness of 'the boss' to give them greater empowerment once their capabilities are in evidence.

Are schools competent to manage their own management development?

All school are competent at something, but some are more competent than others. A significant number of schools are not yet ready to cope with all aspects of their management responsibilities without some support.

There are certainly plenty of sources for advice on competence.

Local education authority consortia and some individual local education authorities already have a wealth of expertise. A report on vocational training (BTEC/CNAA 1990) makes the point that a greater number of people are involved with assessment in competence-based awards than in more conventional programmes of learning. Teachers in schools should not have to travel far to talk to experienced colleagues in other sectors of the education service about competences. Private and public sector enterprises have considerable experience to share with them. Providers of competence based management development programmes for schools and assessment centre providers are also developing effective networks for advice and support. Some professional associations have been active in this field and can also offer advice.

The interest in competence-based management development is spreading to other parts of Europe. Netherlands and Swedish schools are becoming familiar with the use of competence models.

At a meeting in Arnhem in June 1992 the European Forum for Educational Administration established a network to study competence based approaches in the development of educational managers. They are proposing to involve researchers, advisers, providers and school managers with opportunities for exchange of experience and a range of co-development activities. These include:

- a study of approaches to the assessment of management competences, simulations, diagnostic instruments and appraisal systems;
- individual and collective competence development plan formats;
- development activities required for specific management competences;
- validation of competence models used for professional development, appraisal and selection; and
- research and evaluation procedures.

The network has an Arnhem co-ordinator (Drs Charlotte Korbee of Interstudie). It is hoped that this will not prove to be 'a bridge too far' but that the network will stimulate a great deal of interest in competence-based management development. The UK has considerable experience, and a widely varied number of schemes to contribute to the European developments generally.

With all this support available there is no reason why you or your school should not make a start. There are immediate benefits and some sources of help and support. Funding is a problem of course, especially as funds become more fragmented and distributed directly to schools.

A national focus for further progress

It is important to consider the general requirements for school management development. It is clear that there are many potential and actual sources of advice to schools, and that individual teachers are capable of taking ownership of their own development. However things might be better for them if there were national arrangements that supported and monitored management development in schools.

School Management Standards

Proposals have been made for a lead body which would develop competence standards for education. Some of the options are:

- an overall lead body for education, covering all sectors: primary, secondary, further and higher;
- A small executive committee and an operations group with separate working parties to look at primary, secondary, tertiary and higher education sectors; or
- something between the first two options.

The Department for Education and the Department of Employment are considering options at present. There would be advantage in having a set of standards agreed for schools. The projects described in this book illustrate the work done already to identify and use management standards in schools. However, it is important to note the criticism that some experienced managers in industry are making about the Occupational Standards for Managers. It is not so much the standards but the rigid way in which they are being applied that gives cause for concern. There is a tendency to grind everything to grey powder and insist on the achievement of every jot and tittle of the standards. This arises because, if people are to be awarded a national vocational qualification the nation has to be sure that they deserve the award. At present, most teachers like the idea of accreditation but they would not die at the barricades to support a rigidly prescribed NVQ. Nor do most teachers want to use a generic qualification to transfer out of schools. Indeed if they do, we shall have an even greater school management problem!

The advantage of a lead body for education, with a separate working party looking at schools, would be that of putting national resources and effort behind a search for effective School Management Standards at various stages in the teachers career. It might be possible to come up with something rather less rigid, which might still allow teachers to use a variety of competence models in moving towards the achievement of outcomes specified in the School Management Standards. The point has been made that there is only limited use in universal definitions (see Tuxford, in Burke 1989). Each professional field needs to develop its own conception and working definition. Some professions, like school management, are more process than product based and also more context dependent. This is certainly the case in schools, where much of school management is concerned with the management of people (large and small!) and where a governing body or local community may articulate very specific requirements for school management style and behaviour. If generalized competences are developed contextualisation is all the more important (see Wolfe, in Burke 1989).

The personal management portfolio – an entitlement

If schools, as is intended, become more independent of day to day control by intermediate bodies, and as they assert their individual characteristics it will be difficult to sustain a sensible national strategy for career development. The personal management profile, using competence, could provide a career long record of achievement and development for the teachers. Indeed, the portfolio could start during initial teacher training. Some other professions provide management experience as a natural part of initial training. In this way competence based approaches could play their part in providing a coherent career progression for teachers. Competences for classroom management would be a part of a wider competence model that would embrace all aspects of school management. This might help also to emphasize the need in schools for people to develop both the chief executive and leading professional aspects of school leadership (Green 1991). The School Management Task Force advocated a unified career planning and management development scheme for the education service and this could be an important component of it.

Monitoring school management and its development

The new school inspection arrangements will continue the HMI practice of inspecting the effectiveness of school management. A competence-based approach could assist this work. If we have standards for trainers and developers why not standards for inspectors? The new inspection force will no doubt include many people who require more than the initial period of training on offer. A portfolio approach with competence-based development could help to ensure the continued improvement of school inspection standards. Standards for school inspectors should be explicit and available to teachers, governors, parents and the community. In this way an effective inspection service can be developed. In addition for inspectors and school managers and governors to share a common competence framework and language with which to monitor the effectiveness of school management could only help to raise standards and reduce the cynicism about inspection reports which is sometimes prevalent.

Stimulating training and development

A national body should be monitoring and stimulating the development of training and development opportunities for school managers. We have yet to achieve the more comprehensive access to training and development opportunities for all teachers throughout their career which was envisaged by the School Management Task Force. In order to stimulate effective training and development it is necessary to know more about the competences required and the realistic ways in which they can be developed. A national body might also examine the degree to which competence is lost by attrition. I do not suggest that every head should pass an MOT every few years but a national body could give careful thought to the need for reviving and refreshing the competence of experienced but tired managers. This could also be addressed in a national human resource development policy for schools.

Conclusion

The place where management expertise is best developed is in the school. The aim of improving school management is to enhance pupil learning. There is help and advice available to school managers who wish to improve their competence with this ultimate aim in mind. However, time and money will be required if 24,000 service points for the compulsory phase of education are to be effectively managed. The cost of failure is enormous, not only in terms of mismanaged budgets but in terms of lost learning opportunities for young people. The Senior Chief Inspector's comment that 'the management of schools leaves much to be desired' is a warning to those who hold the naive belief that schools can pull themselves up by the bootstraps without advice, support and resources for management development.

Competence based management development can contribute to the improvement of management in the smallest and the largest schools. One school head put it this way. He considered outcomes based work, criterion referenced and outcomes based assessment, records of achievement and profiling and said: 'If such a system is good enough for our pupils then who is to say it is not good enough for us' (Earley 1992).

References

Burke, W. J., (ed), *Competency Based Education and Training*, including contributions by E. Tuxford and A. Wolfe, (Lewes: Falmer Press, 1989).

BTEC/CNAA, *The Assessment of Management Competences*, (Department of Employment (Training), 1990).

Earley, P., *The School Management Competences Project*, (Crawley School, Management South, 1992).

Green, H., 'Strategies for Management Development', in Stevens, D.B. (ed.) *Under New Management* (Harlow: Longman, 1991).

School Management Task Force *Management Development in Schools: the Way Ahead*, (London: HMSO, 1990).

Schroder, H. M., *Managerial Competence: the Key to Excellence*, (Iowa: Kendall Hunt).